SWEEN
TODD

A Victorian Melodrama

by

AUSTIN ROSSER

SAMUEL   FRENCH

LONDON
NEW YORK   TORONTO   SYDNEY   HOLLYWOOD

ISBN 0 573 01516 3

MADE AND PRINTED IN GREAT BRITAIN BY
BUTLER & TANNER LTD, FROME AND LONDON
MADE IN ENGLAND

SWEENEY TODD

Presented at the Dundee Repertory Theatre on 23rd September 1969, with the following cast of characters:

Sweeney Todd	Paul Humpoletz
Tobias Ragg	Alan Bruce
Mark Ingestrie	Michael Stroud
Joanna Oakley	Nell Curran
Dr Aminadab Lupin	James Kennedy
Mrs Lovett	Jenny Burke
Flo	Elizabeth Glenn
Henry	James Kennedy
Jonas Fogg	John Bett
A Labourer	John Bett
Two Men	James Kennedy & Warren Hooper
A Boy	John Bett

Directed by Donald Sartain
Designed by Raymond Lett

ACT I

Scene 1   Sweeney Todd's Barber Shop. Morning, early spring
Scene 2   The alley and streets. That night
Scene 3   Sweeney Todd's shop. The following afternoon

ACT II

Scene 1   The same. That night
Scene 2   Mrs Lovett's Bakehouse. The following afternoon
Scene 3   The same. Several hours later

Time - the early 1840's

NOTE ON THE SETTING

Although a composite setting was used in the Dundee Repertory Theatre production, the play is well suited to separate scene presentation in which simple curtain and/or backcloth settings can be effective.

PRODUCTION NOTE

A serious rather than "comic" treatment of nineteenth-century acting styles is advised.

ACT I

SCENE 1

Sweeney Todd's barber shop, Lovett's bakehouse, (with the pie shop behind it) and the alley beyond. Early spring, 11 a.m.

Tobias Ragg, Sweeney Todd's new apprentice, appears in the street and walks to the barber shop door. He is a small boy, ten years of age, dressed in early-Victorian clothes—boy's cap, short jacket and ankle-length trousers. Under his arm he carries a roll of spare clothing, i.e. a pair of trousers and a shirt. Having looked about him, he knocks on the door and peers through the glass. After a moment he opens the door and enters. Standing on the top step he calls nervously, "Mr Todd—Mr Todd!" There is no reply, and he steps down into the shop, looks about him and walks to the archway. He calls down the corridor, "Mr Todd—it's your new apprentice." No reply. He sits in the barber's chair

After a moment or so Sweeney Todd enters from the corridor. He moves quietly and on seeing Tobias, halts. He is in his late fifties, of tall build and with a tendency to stoop. He wears a white apron over dark woollen cloth knee-breeches and a drab cream-coloured or fawn coarse linen shirt, buckled shoes and black woollen stockings. His hair is plastered down to form an oiled wave or curl over the forehead and his flesh is of pale yet well nourished appearance

Sweeney (*quietly*) And what are yer sitting there for?

Tobias (*jumping to his feet with fright*) I'm the new apprentice, Mr Todd.

Sweeney (*morosely*) Are you! (*He looks him up and down*) And what's yer name?

Tobias Tobias, sir.

Sweeney Tobias what?

Tobias Tobias Ragg, sir—(*adding*)—Mr Todd.

Sweeney Tobias Ragg! (*He takes the bundle from Tobias and throws it under the wash-hand-stand*) Well, Tobias Ragg, I'll give you the benefit of my advice. Loutish ways ain't tolerated 'ere and I'll expect you to show every respect to my customers. (*Taking Tobias by the ear*) And if you want to improve your lot in life learn to study your betters. Study me fads and fancies, for I ain't an easy man to get on with and I have my dark days. (*He releases Tobias' ear and places his hand on the boy's shoulder*) Days when all goes dark and you'll need to find employment outside, for I can't answer for my actions. You understand?

Tobias Yes, sir, Mr Todd.

Sweeney (*pointing to the street*) Have a game of marbles with other lads
or sit on a wall eating a farthing's worth of cake. The pleasures of life
are many. You are fond of life, Tobias Ragg?

Tobias I dunno, Mr Todd.

Sweeney You dunno? That's a strange answer from a boy of your years,
ain't it, Tobias Ragg? Take my advice, you like it—(*he lifts Tobias by
his jacket lapels*)—'cos it ain't very nice to lose it, is it?

Tobias (*nervously*) No, sir.

Sweeney (*letting him down and putting an arm about him*) No. Now you
will remember, Tobias Ragg, I paid ten shillings for you to be my
apprentice, that you have of me board, lodging and washing. Now,
are you not a fortunate, happy dog? What are you?

Tobias A fortunate, happy dog, sir.

Sweeney (*looking steadily at him*) You will acquire a first-rate profession,
quite as good as the law which your mother tells me she would have
put you to, only that a little weakness of the headpiece unqualified you.
(*He pauses*) And now, Tobias, listen.

Tobias (*attentively*) Yes, sir.

Sweeney (*taking the boy's hands*) Your ma told me that you come from
a very "delicate" family, and easily upset, that you've been tenderly
nurtured and you're to be treated as such. Well, you will be, so long
as you don't repeat a word of what passes in this shop. If you do, I'll
cut your throat from ear to ear.

Tobias cries out and tries to pull away

And likewise if you dare to make any supposition, or draw any con-
clusion from anything you may see or hear, or fancy you see or hear.
Do you understand me?

Tobias (*trembling*) I won't say anything, Mr Todd.

Sweeney Are you sure?

Tobias If I do, may I be made into pies at Lovett's in Bell Yard.

Sweeney (*sharply*) Eh, what you mean? (*Pushing Tobias*) What's the idea?
(*Suspiciously*) Do you suspect?

Tobias No, sir, Mr Todd, I don't suspect—indeed I don't. I meant no
harm by the remark.

Sweeney You didn't?

Tobias No, sir. I said the remark in all innocence, sir.

Sweeney (*after a moment*) Good. Very good. I'm satisfied. Quite satisfied.
And mark me, this shop and this shop only is your place 'cept when I
give you the day off.

Tobias (*brightly*) On one of your dark days, sir.

Sweeney (*with a sharp look*) Just you remember. (*After a slight pause*)
And no bibble-babble. And if any customer gives you a penny you can
keep it so that if you get enough of them you'll be a rich man, only I'll
take care of them for you.

*Mark Ingestrie enters the alley, looking about him as if to establish his
whereabouts*

But mark my words, Tobias, life ain't all black, no, it ain't, sometimes it's sunny and you've got a bag of gold in your mit! (*Seeing Mark*) Ah, now there's a seafaring man, Tobias, and one the ladies dote on, I'll be bound. They say it brings 'em good fortune, but they usually get more than they've bargained for.

Tobias What do you mean, sir?

Sweeney Keep a still tongue in your head, for we might have a customer 'ere. (*He opens the door*) Good day, sir! Can I be of any assistance to you?

Mark Ingestrie is a young merchant-seaman of rugged and honest appearance, dressed in a peaked cap, reefer jacket, blue or striped seaman's trousers. He is carrying a small kit-bag containing just a few personal possessions, and speaks with a slight West Country accent

Mark Good day to you, Mr Barber, sir. Do you know the whereabouts of a Miss Joanna Oakley?

Tobias (*running up the steps*) Oh, yes, sir.

Sweeney Who asked you to speak, darling boy? (*He tugs Tobias to the bottom of the steps and clips him*) Another time I'll cut your throat from ear to ear.

Mark Your pardon, sir, I feel I'm to blame for asking the question.

Sweeney (*with a wave of his hand*) No apologies, I beg. Boys will be boys, and a little mild chastisement from time to time does them no harm.

Mark (*nodding*) Perhaps you're right, but I must protest always against unnecessary severity towards young persons. May I ask, sir, if your young lad here knows of Miss Oakley's whereabouts?

Sweeney You may speak, Tobias, darling boy.

Tobias Oh yes, sir. Miss Oakley lives with her parents in Mustard Street.

Sweeney Oh, yes—Mustard Street. Haha.

Mark (*to Sweeney*) Thank you, sir. (*Handing Tobias a coin*) Thank you, "captain", me lad.

Tobias (*looking at Sweeney, then accepting the coin*) Thank you, sir.

Mark You know the lady well?

Tobias She is a kind-hearted lady, sir. For shortly after my father's death, sickness and sorrow overcame my poor mother and myself, and had it not been for Miss Oakley's timely aid, both of us might have perished from want.

Sweeney How it gladdens my heart to hear of such goodness.

Mark And how it gladdens a man's heart to hear his sweetheart so highly esteemed.

Sweeney (*moving Tobias aside*) Indeed, sir, and you are a lucky dog, sir, if I may say so, for the young bloods used to call her the flower of High Street. (*He pauses*) But without wishing to pry, sir, does she not know of your arrival?

Mark (*knocking back his cap*) Thereby hangs a tale, Master Barber. For five years I have forced myself to be absent from this country and the home I love so well. During that time I have promised Mrs Oakley, Joanna's mother, not to communicate with her daughter in any way.

Now the five years are up, and my vessel unexpectedly arriving at this port this morning no sooner do I place my foot on shore but I naturally feel a desire to see her. Judge of my surprise when I discover they are no longer at their former address—but now I am obliged to you both, sir. (*He straightens his cap, nods, and is about to go*)

Sweeney And can I be of any further assistance to you, sir?

Mark Yes, certainly, Mr Barber, sir. (*He leaves his kit-bag on the landing, and hangs his cap on a hook*) It would be churlish of me not to patronize your establishment after the assistance you have given me. And I think a clean face will become the occasion on which I'm embarked. (*He unbuttons his jacket*)

Sweeney Happy to be of service to you, sir. Is it a shave you need? What am I here for but to give you a closer shave than you've ever had before? (*He sharpens his razor on the strop*)

Tobias (*to Mark*) N-no, sir.

Mark does not hear Tobias

Sweeney Tobias, darling boy, show our client to the chair and place a napkin round his neck. (*He takes a napkin from over the back of the chair, shakes it and hands it to Tobias*) Your coat, sir?

Mark (*removing his jacket*) I want it near me, Master Barber. (*Tapping a pocket as he hands it to Sweeney*) This pocket contains an item of value.

Sweeney (*after a short pause*) I see, sir. I'll place it here—(*he puts it on a chair near the wash-stand*) where you can keep an eye on it.

Mark nods

(*Keeping a sharp eye on Tobias*) No doubt a seaman such as yourself, sir, could tell us many a tale of adventure, peril and achievement on the high seas.

Tobias is aware that Sweeney is keeping a close watch on him

Mark (*sitting*) The sea has its perils and its chances, sir.

Tobias places the sheet round Mark

In my time I have been fortunate to amass a thousand pounds, besides becoming the possessor of a string of pearls.

Sweeney (*impressed*) A string of pearls. (*He strops the razor*)

Tobias tries to find opportunities to warn Mark, but occasional glances from Sweeney prevent him from doing so

Tobias (*to Mark; urgently*) Don't! Don't stay, sir! (*He mouths and gesticulates*)

Unable to hear, Mark merely looks puzzled

Sweeney (*turning, but still stropping*) Ah, Toby, my dear. I've suddenly remembered, have you bin to collect Captain Pearson's peruke?

Tobias (*startled*) Captain Pearson's peruke? (*Puzzled*) I don't know, sir.

Sweeney (*no longer stropping*) What do you mean, my darling boy, you don't know? (*To Mark*) He's a little weak in the headpiece, sir. (*Grabbing Tobias*) Captain Pearson's peruke—don't you think you ought to collect it? And on your return the figures of St Dunstan's could well be striking and the exhibition will excite your curiosity and allow me time to shave our customer in peace.

Tobias Please, Mr Todd, can't I stay and lather?

Sweeney (*pushing him to the steps*) No, you can't! Go on, get out! (*He aims a kick at Tobias*)

Tobias steps out of harm's way and exits reluctantly

I'm quite a father to that boy. (*He watches Tobias close the door*) I love him, positively dote on him—so much so, sir, that I feel I could polish him off, in a manner of speaking, haha! Dear me, I'd quite forgotten that you may be in a hurry, sir. (*Brushing Mark's hair*) Just turn your head a little to one side, sir.

Mark does so

Thank you, sir. You were mentioning a string of pearls, sir?

Mark Would you like a glimpse of them, Master Barber?

Sweeney (*delighted, but protesting*) Oh, no, no, no, sir.

Mark Belay awhile, Master Barber, and cast your eyes on some treasures of the East. (*He rises and takes a casket from his jacket pocket*) You see this small casket?

Sweeney (*taking it*) A piece of exquisite workmanship.

Mark (*sitting in the barber's chair*) It's not the box, but the pearls inside should cause you to wonder, for in confidence I tell you they're of the value of twelve thousand pounds.

Sweeney drops the box

Sweeney (*picking up the box, opening it, and marvelling as he holds up the pearls*) Twelve thousand pounds! (*He replaces the pearls and hands the box to Mark with a shudder*) Take them from me, sir, before I'm tempted to steal them from you.

Mark laughs and tosses the box on top of his jacket

(*Shocked and remonstrating*) Oh, no, in your pocket, sir. (*He puts the box in Mark's jacket pocket*) There are some who would commit murder for such a prize. (*He tests the sharpness of the razor*) Ha! Ha! Heugh!

Mark What the devil noise is that?

Sweeney It was only me. I laughed.

Mark Laugh! Hm! Do you call that a laugh? I suppose you caught it off someone who died. If that's your way of laughing I beg you won't do it any more.

Sweeney (*making a lather in his mug*) You will find me all attention to your orders, good sir. Now, sir, we can proceed to business, if it so pleases you. It's well you came here, sir, for though I say it myself, there isn't a shaving shop in the City of London that ever thinks of polishing off a customer as I do—fact, can assure you—ha! Ha! Heugh! Heugh! Heugh!

Mark I'm not of a nervous disposition, Master Barber, but you're making me wonder if I should be sitting in this chair.

Sweeney (*dampening Mark's face*) My apologies, sir. (*After a pause*) You've a very good skin. Ha! Ha! Heugh!

Mark (*annoyed*) Shiver the mainbrace! I'll tell you what it is, Master Barber, if you come that laugh again, I'll get up and go. I don't like it, I tell you, and there's an end of it.

Sweeney Very good, it won't occur again. (*He starts to lather Mark's face*) If I may be so bold, apart from knowing Miss Oakley, have you other acquaintances, relatives, friends—and—and how many people know of your whereabouts at this moment, do you think?

Mark (*jerking his head*) Mind, you'll put the brush in my mouth! You're a mighty curious person, Master Barber, what is it you're after knowing exactly?

Sweeney (*moving to the wash-stand, where he removes the strop and hides it under his apron*) Oh, it's just my way, sir. My apologies, sir. Bless me, where can my strop be? I had it this minute. I must have lain it down somewhere. What an odd thing I can't see it—it's very extraordinary! What can have become of it? Oh, I recollect, I took it in the parlour. Sit still, sir. I shan't be a minute—you can amuse yourself with the news sheet. (*He takes the news sheet from its nail and hands it to Mark*) I'll soon polish you off! Haha! Heugh! Heu . . . (*He stops himself laughing and looks apologetically at Mark*)

Sweeney exits along the corridor

 Mark, irritated, reads the news sheet. Suddenly there is a rumbling sound and a whirring of cog wheels and grating of gear changing. Mark lowers the paper and looks about him with some alarm. The chair tilts forward and part of the stage opens up. Mark yells and calls out, but he is shot out of the chair and disappears completely from view. The chair and floor return to position*

 Sweeney returns, chuckling

When a boy, the thirst of avarice was first awakened in me by the fair gift of a farthing. (*He takes the pearls from Mark's jacket, then goes to the kit-bag*) That farthing soon became a pound—the pound a hundred, and so to a thousand, till I said to myself I will possess a hundred thousand. (*He picks up the bag and holds up the pearls*) This string of pearls will complete the sum! (*He grins at the audience, but is startled by the shop door opening. He hides in the landing corner*)

 Tobias enters cautiously

(*Pouncing on him*) Ahhhh!

* See note and diagram on page 42

Tobias (*terrified*) Noo—ooh!

Sweeney (*with his fist raised*) Speak and speak the truth or your last hour has come! (*He lifts the kit-bag as if to knock Tobias down the steps*)

Tobias, with a yell, runs down the steps. Sweeney follows, carrying the kit-bag and stuffing the pearls in his pocket

How long were you peeping through that door before you came in?

Tobias (*crouching against the wall*) P-p-peeping, sir?

Sweeney Yes, peeping. Don't repeat my words, but answer at once—you'll find it better in the end.

Tobias Please, sir, I wasn't peeping at all.

Sweeney (*with a change of manner*) Well, well, if you did peep, what then? I only wanted to know, that's all. It was quite a joke, wasn't it? Quite funny, though rather odd, eh? Why don't you laugh, you dog? Come now, there's no harm done. (*He puts his finger under the boy's chin*) Tell me what you thought about, eh? (*Smiling*) We'll be merry over it—very merry.

Tobias (*humouring Sweeney*) Yes, very merry, but—(*perplexed*)—I don't know what you mean, sir.

Sweeney I mean nothing at all. Now, sit there, Toby, and tell me all about Captain Pearson's peruke.

Tobias (*sitting*) I don't know where he lives, sir.

Sweeney And you never will, 'cos he don't! (*Sourly*) And in future, when I say collect his peruke, you go and collect it, you understand, Tobias? (*He suddenly glances at the window and calls out in alarm, raising his hands in terror*) Ugh! Ah—aah—what's that?

Tobias, terrified, looks at the window

Haha! Caught you! (*He laughs in triumph*) That made you jump, didn't it? (*He grabs the boy by the lapels of his jacket and with one hand jerks him bodily from the chair*) All nerves, aren't you? What made you 'urry back? Did you think the seafaring man was going to give you another silver joey? Come on! Where is it? (*He puts Tobias down*)

Tobias (*giving the coin to Sweeney*) I was going to give it you, sir.

Sweeney (*pocketing the coin*) Gercha! (*He digs another coin out of his pocket*) Here! I'll give you a farthing for it, and you want to thank yer stars I'm so good and kind.

Tobias (*taking the farthing*) Yes, sir.

Sweeney goes to the corridor and throws Mark's kit-bag and jacket out of sight

Tobias (*observing this*) Has he gone, sir?

Joanna Oakley enters the alley from the street

Sweeney (*sarcastically*) Must 'ave, unless he's dropped down a hole in the floor.

Tobias (*seeing Joanna*) Oh, Mr Todd, there's Miss Oakley!

Sweeney (*looking*) You didn't go searching for her, did you?

Tobias (*with his face averted*) No, sir.

Sweeney (*with a change of manner*) And why not, eh? Why shouldn't you have?

Joanna enters the shop, closing the door. She is an attractive young woman in the early twenties, dressed in bonnet, simple crinoline type of dress, and cloak

Good morning, Miss Oakley. What a pleasure it is to feast my eyes on your beauteous face.

Joanna Good morning, Mr Todd.

Sweeney And what can I do for you, my dear?

Joanna I am looking for a gentleman, Mr Todd.

Sweeney And what might the gentleman's name be, Miss Oakley?

Joanna Mark Ingestrie, Mr Todd.

Sweeney (*savouring the name*) Mark Ingestrie! What a pretty name! And might this gentleman be a seafaring man?

Joanna Oh, Mr Todd, my informant was correct then. Mr Ingestrie has called here?

Sweeney (*glancing at Tobias*) Your informant?

Joanna Yes. Mr Fogg, the asylum superintendent, told me that a gentleman answering Mark's description came here.

Sweeney And he was quite correct, though what business it is of that tub of lard—I don't know. My apologies, my dear, but he's a gent I've little time for. But your Mr Ingestrie has already left—but a few minutes ago—eagerly hastening his steps towards your house in Mustard Street. No doubt at this moment he's being shown into the parlour to await your return.

Joanna (*turning to depart*) Dear Mr Todd, thank you so much.

Sweeney Good-bye, my dear.

Joanna (*seeing Mark's cap hanging on the peg*) Look, Mr Todd, a seaman's cap—could that be Mr Ingestrie's?

Sweeney (*taking the cap from the peg*) I believe it could be. He must have forgotten it in his haste to see you. Perhaps you will kindly return it to him.

Joanna Yes, of course, Mr Todd.

Sweeney Tobias, my dear boy, escort Miss Oakley down the street. Good-bye once again, Miss Oakley.

Joanna Good-bye, Mr Todd.

Tobias opens the door, and he and Joanna make their way along the street, Tobias closing the door after them

Sweeney (*waving after them through the window*) Good-bye! Good-bye! Tata! (*He turns to the audience*) Oooh, I'd like to cut her throat—more than I could do to keep my hands off it! I could have a bit of fun, finishing her off behind a blackberry bush. I'll take the rest of the day off and await my opportunity to get her on her own. (*He bolts the shop* *door*) You never know what Fate has in store, especially when the moon is high. I'll hang about the streets and alleys and passages and footpaths tonight. There are plenty of dark places I can grab 'old of her and drag her into. Oooh, haha! I must be careful not to let my excitement get the better of me!

A Labourer comes and shakes the shop door

Labourer Ain't you open, then, Mr Tod?
Sweeney (*turning and scowling*) No. I'm closed.

CURTAIN

SCENE 2

That night.

The alley is lit by a street-lamp. No light—or very little—spills into the bakehouse or the shop. It is moonlight and there is mist in the air. The moaning of a not-so-distant ship's hooter indicates the presence of fog

Dr Aminadab Lupin enters and walks down the alley, then takes a brandy flask from his pocket and drinks. He is a tall, lean man about fifty years of age. He wears a long dark cloak, and a top hat: under the cloak a preacher's suit, a white collar and black cravat. His trousers fit closely to the calf and over the top of his light-weight boots by means of elastic running under the instep

Lupin (*glancing back up the alley*) And so, Miss Oakley, truly I believe thou to be one of the foolish virgins; if thou thinkst that I—Aminadab Lupin, Doctor of Divinity, preacher extraordinary to all the best families should—(*breaking off*)—families of no small means and substance— should condescend to offer my help in thy search for a common sailor and my rival to thy hand, to boot, then in truth, thou art a foolish one. (*He drinks*) Why shouldst I search for your scurvy, libidinous Romeo who hast no doubt dallied with disease and providers of man's bodily needs in every flesh house from the frozen North to the tropical South. How canst thou compare a man of his ordinary parts to me, a man of superior mould—both in religion and sensuality—who hast made virgins tremble in every church throughout the land? Hast thou not yet seen the light of lust—I mean piety—in my eye? For indeed, thy mother Mistress Oakley has. Thy mother dotes on me and my charm, and pants for more of me and wishes increasingly every day for me to to be her son-in-law. But peace, Eros! Oho, peace! (*He drinks*) My corrupt and lascivious appetite—or do I mean saintly and temperate— ho, ho? Ha, ha!—grows large on pleasure delayed and yet tonight, who

knows? I may have my way with the fair Joanna. Hark, hark! (*He listens*)
O peace, Eros, thou monster. (*Excitedly*) I hear the murmurings of my
turtle-dove approaching. (*He moves into the darkness*)

Joanna enters

Joanna (*dabbing her eyes*) Oh, Mark, Mark. Why have you deserted me
in this late hour of our relationship? I have relied so abundantly on your
true lasting affection. (*She pauses*) Why haven't you sent me some token
of your existence and of your eternal love? The merest, slightest word
that you are still alive would be sufficient.

Lupin coughs

Who is that?
Lupin (*appearing and moving to Joanna*) Only Aminadab helping you to
search for Mr Ingestrie, my dear Joanna. Mayhap thou wouldst find
solace and comfort in partaking in a communal thought with me, a
moment's prayer together here in the moonlight.
Joanna No, thank you, Aminadab. I think we should continue our
search.
Lupin (*scornfully*) You appreciate he's a common sailor whose affections
are as chaff in the wind? You have no certain knowledge of his devotion.
Joanna (*quietly and with conviction*) Only an inner feeling, Aminadab.
But what is of greater moment is that today I feel—(*disturbed*)—I
hesitate to say it—something terrible has happened to Mark.
Lupin At the barber Todd's, you mean?
Joanna Yes.
Lupin (*emphatically*) If Mr Ingestrie has disappeared 'tis because he has
chosen to. (*After a pause*) Because he wishes to assume a fresh identity
so that he can bigamously marry yet another well set up virgin.
Joanna (*coldly*) I think not, Aminadab.
Lupin (*placing his hands on her shoulders*) What dost thou know of life,
innocent trembling girl? Aah, many such as thou die of shame on their
wedding night.

Joanna moves away from him

Thy noble mariner—(*following her*)—has experienced fleshly shame to
a degree that wouldst hurl thee into convulsions of disgust. What dost
thou know, trembling innocent—(*darkly*)—of man the beast?
Joanna I have no liking for conversations of this nature, Aminadab.
Lupin (*holding out his arms*) You must be saved from the lustful bellowings
of the male brute. Seek refuge in my arms and participate in spiritual
wedlock with my pure soul and body. O! Thou lamb of innocence
placed on the altar of carnal sacrifice. (*Kneeling*) I cannot bear the
thought! I must ravish you. . . . (*he corrects himself*) I mean, I must
marry you as soon as possible.

Joanna moves past him up the alley

Where are you going?

Joanna When you asked to accompany me on this search for Mr Ingestrie, you promised that you would not take advantage of the situation to molest me with doubtful protestations.

Lupin moves to prevent her moving away

You have broken that promise, and you will allow me, Dr Lupin . . . (*She breaks off*) No! No more can I address thee as Aminadab—you will allow me to continue on my way unaccompanied.

Lupin (*not moving*) Disrespectful virgin! (*Taking her hands in his*) You do not fully understand the position which would be yours if you married me. Allow me to add that your mother most certainly wishes for such a union between us and is completely against your marrying anyone else—particularly a common seaman!

Joanna (*snatching her hands away*) My mother's wish is not necessarily mine, Dr Lupin.

Lupin Thy mother hath decided that I must force thee to my bosom as a wedded wife!

Joanna (*outraged*) You have been drinking, Dr. Lupin!

Lupin I never drink except when the spirit waxeth faint. (*He takes the flask from his pocket and drinks*) 'Tis an ungodly practice! (*He drinks again*) Thou wilt shortly become as bone of my bone, flesh of my flesh. (*He puts the flask in his pocket and suddenly seizes her*) Thou dost deserve such an honour.

Joanna (*struggling*) We don't receive all we deserve in this world, I hope, Dr Lupin.

Lupin (*pulling her to him*) But, my dear, we must try to be happy; 'tis a sin to be miserable and an even greater sin to cause it in others.

Joanna I would not disagree!

Lupin (*with one hand untying her bonnet and trying to push it off her head*) Yet you refuse to make me happy!

Joanna (*desperately*) I do not love you!

Lupin (*unfastening her cloak*) Think of how I could help your parents— perhaps you do not know that I've gained wealth by various means.

She succeeds in catching him off balance and pushing him away

Aah, don't think I'll let you go so easily, I'm not the man to fail in my purpose. (*He grabs her cloak and tugs it from her*)

Joanna (*seeking to dodge round him*) In this you will, for believe me, sir, you are nothing but a toad!

Lupin (*gritting his teeth*) Toad? You call a man who loves you—a toad?

Joanna Yes, indeed, and a lecherous one, moreover.

Lupin (*spreading the cloak on the ground and keeping an eye on Joanna*) Am I? Am I? Well, since you think so, that I'll be!

He makes a sham move to leap across the cloak at her and tricks her into running round it into his arms

Joanna Unhand me, sir!

Lupin (*holding her in a bear hug*) Haha! Trapped! You'll be my swooning
spouse, whether you wish it or not! And if you won't accept me as a
gentle suitor I'll force you to the ground here by the wayside. Eh? Let
us lie down on this cloak and settle the matter.

Joanna Never! Never! You beast!

Lupin (*grabbing her wrists and forcing her to her knees*) I have lain awake
at nights with an image of you in my mind—and I have imagined you
in your night attire and then—naked—on your bed! Haha!

Joanna (*in pain as he increases the pressure on her wrists*) No—no!

Lupin I have drawn your form in the snow and melted it with my breath!
You spurn me—but once I've ploughed the field and sown the seed
you'll come crawling to me to marry you and save you from disgrace.

Joanna (*with spirit and defiance*) I am already on my knees!

Lupin Soon to be on your back.

They struggle

Joanna Never! Never! Never!

Lupin (*raising her arms back over her head so that she is forced down on
her back*) Resist not! I'm as a magnet drawn to a loadstone and we
shall lie together. (*Kneeling beside her recumbent form*) I am in an agony
of passion and I shall ease the pain with the moisture of your ruby lips!

Joanna (*pleading*) No!

Lupin Nay, I'm resolved. (*He lies beside her and kisses her mouth and neck*)
Ah! Ah! (*Raising his head; ecstatically*) Oh, you spirited slut! (*He presses
down on her again*)

A laugh is heard off

What's that? We must not be caught at it! (*He listens and decides it is
wise to get to his feet*) Who is there? Who comes along?

Sweeney appears out of the darkness

Sweeney It is I, Sweeney Todd, taking a stroll. I'm looking for Miss
Oakley. Have you seen her?

Lupin (*straightening his clothes*) Why yes, she is here, passing the time of
evening with me.

Joanna rises and gathers her bonnet and cloak

Sweeney (*observing her*) Oh, would you excuse me, Mr Lupin, but I'd
like to discuss one or two matters privately with Miss Oakley. (*To the
audience*) I've got my razor to polish her off! (*To Lupin*) You'll excuse
us, Lupin? (*To Joanna*) My dear, would you care to take my arm and
walk a little way with me?

Joanna is petrified and recoils from Sweeney

Lupin (*after a slight pause*) Certainly. I'll leave you. But *Doctor* Lupin,
if you please, Mr Todd.

Sweeney Thank you—(*he pauses*)—Lupin. Good night.

Lupin goes up the alley and off

Was old Lupin annoying you? I'm glad I came along. I'd hate to see such a charming neck—(*touching her*)—rudely touched by him!

Joanna Please, Mr Todd . . .

Sweeney Yes, my dear?

Joanna Don't touch my neck!

Sweeney (*withdrawing his hand*) Sorry, my dear.

Joanna I can find my own way home, Mr Todd.

Sweeney (*letting her pass him, then taking her arm*) I'm afraid I can't allow you to go home unescorted! (*Searching for his razor*) Is that the Pole Star up there?

Joanna Why do you ask such a question?

Sweeney I wanted to see you lift your head towards the sky.

Joanna Why?

Sweeney So that I might see your neck outlined against the night.

Joanna Mr Todd, your voice and what you say are strange.

Sweeney Are they, my dear?

Joanna (*after a pause*) What have you in your hand? It glints! (*Catching her breast*) Mr Todd, don't come any nearer!

Sweeney You suspect too much! (*He lifts the razor in the air*)

Joanna seizes his razor arm and holds it away from her, screaming in terror as she does so. Sweeney with his free arm pulls her around backwards against him. Lupin enters unseen

You suspect too much!

Joanna (*screaming*) No! No!

Lupin (*from the darkness*) Excuse me, Mr Todd . . . (*He breaks off as he sees Sweeney leap back with surprise*)

Joanna rushes off in panic and sobbing

Can I visit you at your famous establishment tomorrow?

Sweeney (*gazing after Joanna's retreating form, hissing through his teeth and tutting*) Sssh! Sssh! Tch! Tch! (*After a moment he shrugs, laughs coldly, and turns to Lupin. Pocketing his razor*) But, of course, Lupin. At your service, sir.

Lupin smiles and Sweeney smiles back, as—

the CURTAIN *falls*

B

Scene 3

The following afternoon
As the Curtain *rises, Mrs Lovett enters Sweeney's shop carrying a mug of tea and a meat pie on a tray. She goes to close the door, when a Boy pops his head round the top end of the alley*

Boy (*calling*) I want two tuppeny pies for Mrs Widdle Waddle!
Mrs Lovett (*shouting back*) Oh, go away! I'm not going back to my place just for you! Go on! Go away!

The Boy pulls a face at her and goes

(*Indignantly*) Oooh, I saw you! How rude! Wait till I see your parents! (*As an afterthought*) If you have any! (*Closing the door*) Urchin! (*She walks down the steps with the tray*)

Mrs Lovett is a big woman in her late forties or early fifties. She has strong forearms and a florid complexion. She is wearing a mobcap, but the hair which can be seen appears frizzed and artificially coloured. Her dress is of drab colour and long-skirted, with a couple of layers of petticoat showing. Her shoes are low-heeled. She is also wearing a large and rather grubby apron and a bright-coloured kerchief across the shoulders

(*Carrying the tray to the wash-stand*) Heigho! (*She sighs*) I feel lonely. That's why I've brought Mr Todd a little snack so that I can share my loneliness with him. I've been proper lonely since Mr Lovett died. I really ought to marry one of my many admirers. I wonder what the prospects of Major Bounce are? He's tolerably good-looking, although middle-aged. Then there's Aminadab Lupin, a very nice man but a little holy, holy for me. (*She sees someone at the shop door*) Oooh, there's someone coming! (*She takes the hand-mirror from the wash-stand and glances in it*) Wonder what I look like? (*She quickly replaces it*)

Lupin enters the shop

Why, Mr Lupin, I do declare! How strange and fascinating!

Lupin hangs up his hat, gloves and cloak, and puts his stick in the container

I've just been thinking of you—ah ha! (*Wagging her finger playfully*) You are well, I hope?
Lupin So, dear sister, you're given to thinking of me, eh? But my mood today is one of melancholy! Let's hope, sister, that your sufferings here will in a future world be changed to peace and happiness. (*With his hand raised*) Yea, verily, and I say unto you, the acts of the wicked shall call forth the wrath they deserve!
Mrs Lovett (*confused*) Oh, la! (*Nodding agreement*) Yes, yes, of course.
Lupin (*looking at her severely*) Are you a wicked woman?

Mrs Lovett Pardon?

Lupin Are you a wicked woman?

Mrs Lovett (*worried, and after a pause deciding to confess*) Oh, dear Mr Lupin—(*going on her knees*)—how did you guess? No! What am I saying? (*Rising; hurriedly*) No, I'm not really wicked. No, of course I ain't.

Lupin I wish I could say that of our dear brother, Todd—what know you of his evil, sister?

Mrs Lovett Oh Lord, Mr Lupin dear—*Doctor* Lupin dear, I should say —don't question me about that man! All I know is that *I* ain't wicked. Not wicked in any way.

Lupin (*taking her hand and patting it*) Dear sister, you are indeed an angel! (*Noticing the mug of tea*) And moreover, you are a blessing just as tea is a blessing, dear sister. What should we do without it?

Mrs Lovett Indeed, 'tis a blessing, Dr Lupin.

Lupin (*placing her arm around his waist*) Call me brother, dear sister, for we are all brothers and sisters in this wicked world, are we not?

Mrs Lovett (*thrilled*) Oh, Dr Lupin, may I? (*Coyly*) I've felt so lonely all day wishing Dr Lupin might pass by.

Lupin Yes, *tea* is a blessing, dear sister.

Mrs Lovett (*putting her other arm round his waist*) Ah indeed, 'tis a blessing, Dr Lupin—(*adding bashfully*)—brother.

Lupin (*glancing at the tea*) Yes.

Mrs Lovett (*suddenly understanding*) Oh—would you like a mug? It is Mr Todd's. I brought it specially for him.

Lupin (*chucking her under the chin*) You are a woman of kindness, dear— (*after a pause*)—Lily.

Mrs Lovett giggles

No wonder I've often heard common working fellows call you the lovely Lovett.

Mrs Lovett (*simpering and giggling*) Oooh, oh la! Ha! Ha! Oh, oh, ho, ho! Ha! Do they now? (*Breaking away and bringing him the mug of tea*) Look, you have this mug of tea, never mind Mr Todd, he should not be away so long.

Lupin Nay, sister, I cannot deprive him.

Mrs Lovett Oh pray, brother Lupin, do!

Lupin takes the mug

What else do they say of me?

Lupin They say you are the soul of kindness and that you are very wealthy —Lily.

Mrs Lovett (*moving close to him and putting his arm about her*) Draw a little closer, brother.

Lupin And is it true, dear sister, that thou hast gathered to thyself much of the mammon of unrighteousness by the sale (*breaking from her and moving to the tray*) of these same pieces of manna which the ungodly call dough, wrapped round the flesh of the fatted calf? (*He points at the pie*)

Mrs Lovett (*coyly*) Oh, Doctor-brother, what a lovely way of saying pies.
Lupin (*sitting*) Call me brother, dear sister, verily 'doctor-brother'' is an
abomination. And thou sayest, there is much of the mammon of unrighteousness in what thou callest pies? Thou hast what the wicked call
a stocking?
Mrs Lovett Oh la! Brother, thank you! They are rather nice. (*She looks
at her legs*)
Lupin Nay, sister, I mean a stocking hidden away in which you save
money?
Mrs Lovett (*becoming cautious and moving away*) Nay, let's not talk of
that nor pies. (*Peevishly*) Remember, that all day and all night I think
of nothing but pies, and sometimes pies haunt my dreams; remember
that all day I smell pies and knead dough for pies and take tuppences
for pies!
Lupin Verily, sister, it is a delicious text: Lo, the smell of gravy haunteth
my nostrils, and my soul quivers with delight! (*He places his hand on her
hip*)
Mrs Lovett (*delighted*) Then would you like a pie, brother?
Lupin My soul fainteth, yea, my stomach crieth out, oh my sister, oh
my——

Mrs Lovett holds the pie temptingly in front of him

——beloved, verily I would partake of thy pies! (*He takes the offered pie
and begins to eat it*) Nay, sister, of a surety, this is not a tuppenny pie?
Mrs Lovett No, Mr Lupin, that is a very special pie, a pie such as I keep
for callers and friends.
Lupin (*sitting in the barber's chair*) And tell me, sister—(*he chews the pie*)
—there is great profit on a tuppenny pie? Dost thou put in a pennyworth
of the fat of the calf?
Mrs Lovett (*watching him eat*) A ha'porth, Mr Lupin.
Lupin And whence comest thy flour, my beloved?
Mrs Lovett I buy it from Miller Brown.
Lupin And Miller Brown has nearby his mill certain cavities in the earth
containing chalk, hath he not, sister?
Mrs Lovett (*resenting this*) Miller Brown is a highly respectable merchant,
Dr Lupin.
Lupin Hoity toity! Did I say aught else? (*He finishes eating the pie*) Ah,
sister, what a pie, what a pie was that! Behold, my heart yearneth after
thy beauty: behold a great love welleth up in my soul! (*He burps*) Wilt
thou take my hand? (*He pulls her to him so that she sits on his knee*)
And hast thou a stocking, eh? Hark now, I will whisper, is it near thy
bed?
Mrs Lovett (*playfully slapping his hand*) Brother, brother, you mustn't!
Dr Lupin, you are a naughty man.
Lupin Hist, my beloved. I yearn to be fruity! (*He kisses her*) Wilt call me
Lupy now? And wilt meet me at twelve o'clock near Temple Bar? For
the work of the Lord calleth his servant and I must begone. (*Whispering*)
Twelve o'clock near Temple Bar?

Mrs Lovett (*pleased, but deciding to be more difficult to catch*) Now, now, why should I? (*She removes his hands and stands*) I won't say yes and I won't say no.

Lupin (*holding out his arms*) Please, lovely Lovett, do! (*He suddenly looks about him as if he has heard something, then stands and moves close to Mrs Lovett, his voice and manner tense*) Lily—Lily—(*with another quick glance about him*)—can someone overhear us?

Mrs Lovett (*alert*) What? What? (*Looking about her*) What do you mean, Lupy?

Lupin Can anyone overhear?

Mrs Lovett (*nervously*) I don't think so. (*She peers down the corridor to make sure no-one is there*) Why?

Lupin I feel there is someone close at hand watching us. . . .

There is a pause. They listen

Mrs Lovett Oh, brother, are you not afraid of him, Mr Sweeney Todd?

Lupin (*confidently*) I'm a clever man, sister, I have no need to fear him.

Mrs Lovett Oh, Lupy, 'tis because of Todd that I can't be sure if I should meet you. He's a dangerous man!

Lupin Has he secret powers over you?

Mrs Lovett No, no, none! (*Nearing despair*) Oh, I'm so afraid of him! Yes, yes, what you suggest is true. (*She holds herself, her bosom heaving and palpitating*) Oh, my heart's in my mouth—I'll die of fear—I'm throbbing all over. (*After a pause*) He has knowledge of me I don't wish others to know!

Lupin (*soothingly*) Lovely Lily, he's a danger to you. (*Holding her gently to him*) No-one can hear or see us. (*He pauses*) Do you know of any wicked deed of which Sweeney Todd is guilty?

Mrs Lovett (*breaking away*) Ah, don't ask me such questions! Don't! Don't! You are not to question me about Todd. He'll kill us both. We must be careful.

Lupin (*patting her shoulder*) There, there, lovely, you'll be safe. If we meet tonight, you'll tell me then, eh? Twelve o'clock. I want to see that stocking of yours. . . .

Mrs Lovett (*embracing him*) Oh, Lupy!

Lupin (*eagerly*) You will?

Mrs Lupin (*to the audience*) I must tell someone for I'm going mad with the knowledge of it. (*To Lupin*) Lupy, will you help me get rid of Sweeney Todd—put the law on him—for in truth until he is dead never shall I be free. Will you, Lupy?

Lupin (*holding out his arms as if to keep some distance between them in order to think clearly*) Yes, yes, verily I believe this Sweeney to be a man of sin. (*He creeps quickly but warily to see that there is no-one in the corridor, then inspects the room with a number of glances about him*) Yea, I believe he has secrets that he will buy at a great price. It is said that his wealth is very great.

Mrs Lovett 'Tis so.

Lupin Aye, truly, it is only just that the wicked like him should be robbed.

And until we have made a little money from him it is not profitable to place him in the hands of the law. Do you agree?

Mrs Lovett Ah, you're a clever one, Fruity—I mean Lupy—you give me fresh hope. We'll rob the monster first!

Lupin (*quietly*) We are together in this, eh?

She nods agreement

But no more discussion until tonight! (*Raising a finger*) Sssh! (*He takes the mug from the tray and drinks*)

Sweeney is seen standing outside the shop door

Mrs Lovett (*terrified, beginning to shake, and placing her hand on her stomach*) Oooh, I feel awful! My liver and lights—ooh—ooh . . .

Lupin (*acting unconcerned*) Indeed, it was delicious pastry.

Sweeney enters and closes the shop door, walking down the steps looking at them both

Mrs Lovett (*trying to sound unconcerned*) Pleased you appreciated it, Dr Lupin.

Sweeney If it isn't my old friends Mrs Lovett and Lupin. I've just been strolling through the graveyard. What a lovely day it is.

Lupin Most pleasant, Todd.

Sweeney What can I do for you, Lupin? (*He removes his tail-coat and hat and ties on his apron*)

Lupin Believe it or not, Todd, I would have you shave me.

Sweeney Certainly. After that bracing walk I feel I could shave the whole of England. But you, my dear Mrs L., what can I do for you?

Mrs Lovett I came to pass the time of day with you; bringing one of my best pies and something to wash it down with—but Dr Lupin here, I'm afraid, has had it!

Sweeney (*looking meaningfully at Lupin*) Oh?

Mrs Lovett I'll bring you along something extra to make up for it.

Sweeney Fair dame, don't inconvenience yourself! I'll be feeling peckish when I've shaved our friend Lupin, and then I'll come across and see you. Ta! Ta! Till then! (*Dismissing her with a wave*) Bye, bye.

Mrs Lovett Yes, Mr Todd. I'll hurry off, then.

Mrs Lovett goes out of the shop and into her pie-shop

Lupin Charming woman!

Sweeney She has money, too. But she ain't as tasty as the little tasty wench I saw you "accompanying" the other night.

Lupin Tush, tush, you have the wickedest mind! My feelings for that virgin are as pure as the driven snow. (*After a slight pause*) But soon after I went I heard a scream ripped off by the wind. Why was that, I wonder?

Sweeney She thought she heard you coming back!

Lupin But what was that shiny object in your hand, Mr Todd?

Sweeney I was persuading the young lady to kiss me!

Lupin As indeed was I the moment you arrived. Oh, the world is wicked.

Sweeney (*taking the mug from Lupin*) O, 'tis. Give us a drink of your tea! (*He drinks, then proffers it back to Lupin*) Have some?

Lupin (*taking the mug and having a sip*) Many thanks, brother. Tell me, how does she manage to make her pies so tasty?

Sweeney Who?

Lupin Mrs Lovett.

Sweeney 'Tis because she's a good cook, that's why.

Lupin Tell me, Todd, do you think her a strange woman? There is an evil about her, brother, think you not? (*He puts the mug on the tray*)

Sweeney (*as Lupin puts the mug down; to the audience*) What's the fool up to?

Lupin I could hardly bear talking to the creature, I thought her so odious.

Sweeney You ate her pie.

Lupin She had to be humoured, Todd. But now, sir, a fine shave, if you please.

Sweeney Certainly. Pray sit down. (*He stands back from the barber's chair*)

Lupin steps cautiously over to the chair and sits

Lupin And where do you purchase a chair such as this, Todd?

Sweeney (*wrapping a napkin round Lupin and then picking up his lather mug*) Don't know. Just found it one morning. (*Muttering*) I wonder if I should polish him off?

Lupin What do you say?

Sweeney Where do you usually go for a shave? (*Applying the lather vigorously*) Shave yourself, do you?

Lupin Please, please, Todd, not so vigorous!

Sweeney You weren't coming about here to enquire about a young fellow named Ingestrie by any chance?

Lupin Never heard of the young man, Todd.

Sweeney (*stopping lathering for a moment*) Haven't you, now? Haven't you?

Lupin No.

Sweeney Miss Oakley never mentioned him?

Lupin Now, let me think. (*After a pause*) No. Never.

Sweeney (*lathering*) I thought you might be doing a little of her searching for her.

Lupin What relation is the young man to her?

Sweeney Her lover, Lupin.

Lupin Now why should I be searching for him, Todd?

Sweeney (*placing the mug on the stand and picking up the razor*) Because you're so good and kind.

Lupin Do you know anything about him, Todd?

Sweeney Lupin—(*he pauses*)—how much would you pay for that young man to die?

Lupin Only kind fate could do that!

Sweeney (*starting to strop the razor*) I'm a clever man. I think I can accomplish all that fate can! -

Lupin (*gazing at Todd*) Oh, yes, really, Todd. Most interesting.

Sweeney (*pausing in his stropping*) Yes, I could. For a little gift of money.

Lupin (*casually*) How much?

Sweeney Two hundred pounds.

Lupin (*rising*) Well, I would like five times that amount from you, Sweeney Todd!

Sweeney (*rather astonished*) What's that?

Lupin You heard me distinctly, Todd. Five times that amount!

Sweeney Why?

Lupin For not mentioning certain suspicions.

Sweeney (*putting down the razor*) Wait! (*He raises his hand significantly, goes to the door, glances through it, then locks it. Then he wipes his hand on his apron and holds it out to Lupin*) Let me grasp your hand! Come here, you religious humbug, for Sweeney Todd to grasp your hand.

Lupin goes and shakes hands with Sweeney

You've snooped and snooped until you've found me out! Well, you mustn't expect that much from me. I can't afford that much!

Lupin I'm sure you can.

Sweeney No, I assure you. I know you have caught me——

Lupin withdraws his hand

——but it's no good squeezing too hard. Ha! Ha! Come, I'm big enough to admire your cunning! (*He places his hands on Lupin's shoulders*) It's equal to me own. (*He removes one hand, and with the other leads Lupin over to the wash-stand*) Now, you be generous and ask for a smaller sum. Or at least come to some other arrangement.

Lupin No, I don't think so. I'd like a little now, Mr Todd.

They eye each other

Sweeney (*after a pause*) Certainly, excuse me, Lupin. (*He moves Lupin from the table*) I'll pay you! (*He opens the drawer in the wash-stand and takes out a black velvet bag. He pours some jewels on to the palm of his hand and shows them to Lupin*)

Lupin is amazed

Surprised I have so much, are you?

Lupin (*after gazing his fill; trying to appear nonchalant*) Where did you get all this?

Sweeney From my customers. They pay well, don't they?

Lupin And now you can pay me the small amount I first asked for!

Sweeney What, a thousand pounds?

Lupin That was the sum.

Sweeney (*putting the jewels in the bag*) Pish! You can have more than that. Far more.

Lupin What?

Sweeney Here! Take these! (*He tosses the bag of jewels to Lupin*)

Sweeney exits, but returns immediately with a large jewel box

Lupin takes one or two jewels from the box and studies them closely. He watches Sweeney when the latter, on his return, throws back the lid of the box and takes out ropes of pearls and one or two ruby necklaces and other pieces of jewellery

(*quietly*) You know many kinds of people, you're a man of subtle influence. You could find out the men who carry a lot of wealth—who have few prying relatives—men who won't be missed much—and introduce them to my establishment.

Lupin puts the jewels back in the bag as he listens

Between us we would gain enough wealth in two years to live as lords in golden palaces. Here! Look at 'em! (*He pushes the ropes of pearls, etc., at Lupin*) Go on! Touch 'em!

Lupin (*almost choking with delight as he examines them*) Oooh, oh, ah, aah! But now tell me, how do you manage?

Sweeney To polish them off?

Lupin (*nodding*) To polish them off!

Sweeney Ha! Ha! (*He takes the black bag from Lupin, picks up the jewel box and deposits them on a chair*) Now you watch! I say, "Good day, sir!" (*He walks to the door pretending a customer has entered the shop*)

Lupin follows behind Sweeney, enjoying the "entertainment"

"Certainly, sir. No, not that chair, sir, this one. The light is better, sir, and it's more comfortable!" And they sit like this. (*He sits in the barber's chair, still pretending*)

Lupin gets caught up in the fun

Get the brush!

Lupin does so and starts to lather Sweeney

Don't you tickle! Oh, ha! Ha! Ha! Ha! It tickles! Now the razor! Get it quick!

Lupin goes for the razor

Then when you're sitting comfortably, somethin' horrible happens. You'd never think anything was. Have you ever shaved anyone? Get the razor, man! It's sharp! Now slide it gently down my skin.

Lupin does so

Ah, yes. One would never think anything was going to happen. Tell me, would you suspect?

Lupin (*handing Sweeney the razor*) Let me try.

Sweeney (*handing Lupin the sheet*) Put this round you! (*He swiftly takes* *a noosed rope from under the wash-stand and throws it over Lupin from behind. As he binds Lupin to the chair)* Aha, my little bird—caught!

Lupin But I'm your partner.

Sweeney *(behind the chair)* But you are, my dear Tulip—I mean Lupin— you still are, for ten seconds. *(He gets the brush and lather mug)* Now I'll lather you. Oh, you've a very good skin. *(He returns the mug and brush and picks up the razor)* A very good skin. The razor is going over it like a slender skater. You know, when I go near the neck I want to draw my razor across it—like a violin. Isn't it strange—and there are no musicians in the family. *(He starts to sing)* "Oh, 'tis a tulip stem I draw my blade across—balade across!"

Lupin Please, please! *(Hoping to humour Sweeney)* Ha, ha, don't joke.

Sweeney I'm not. I usually slit 'em in the cellar. There are a number there now; some of 'em dead, some of 'em almost dead—it's a terrible long drop to the cellar, you know—waiting to go to the lovely Lovett. For your next stop, mate, is the pie factory!

Lupin *(imploring)* No, no, Todd, please.

The LIGHTS *begin to dim*

Sweeney *(quietly)* So now, partner, you know everything—*(slowly)*— everything you were snooping to find out from Lovett. I was listening you know.

The LIGHTS *are now so low that only the outlines of the figures can be seen*

So this is where our partnership ends. *(He cuts Lupin's throat)*

The LIGHTS *come up to half full. Lupin is seen dead in the chair, his head dropping forward. Sweeney, with the open razor in his hand, comes down and speaks to the audience*

As a little child I used to cut the flowers with Granny's scissors in her sunlit garden. Oh, oh, I wish the whole world were a throat so that I could cut it!

CURTAIN

ACT II

Scene 1

That night
A small card table has been set up in one corner of Sweeney Todd's shop
Tobias enters, looking for a blanket

Tobias Oh, I'm so cold. I wish I could find myself a blanket. (*He searches on the landing to see if any cloaks have been left there, but finds nothing*) Oh dear. (*He turns and peers down into the shop*) I wonder if Miss Oakley will find that seaman and then bring me some clothes.

A creaking noise is heard

What's that? (*He listens, his hair seeming to stand on end as he witnesses what happens*) Oooh, what is it?

*Slowly the chair and trapdoor rise and a wounded Mark Ingestrie cautiously climbs out and looks about him. He wears a grubby tweed jacket**

Mark (*searching about the room*) Have my senses left me? Do I dream of horrors unparalleled or is my existence a reality? I remember this place—the man who shaved me stood yonder, and this is the chair on which I sat, afterwards falling into the depths below. (*He goes to the chair and investigates. It moves—either up and down on the trap or into the wall on a runner system*) Heavens! This is a contrivance for the purpose of murder and robbery! (*He puts his hands to his head in amazement as he realizes what has happened*) My pearls—lost! (*Grimly*) The facts are clear enough. The owner of this shop is a robber and murderer. But I haven't quite fallen a victim to his designs yet; for though feeling weak and defenceless I'll sell my life dearly. (*He pauses*) I can hear breathing! (*Quietly*) There's someone here! The murderer himself! Who's here? Eh? Where are you? The sound is up here . . . (*He discovers Tobias in a corner and pulls him into the light*) Who are you? What are you doing here?

Tobias Please let me go!

Mark That I won't. Come on, speak up. (*He shakes him*)

Tobias I'm Tobias Ragg, Mr Todd's apprentice. Don't you remember me.

Mark Yes, I do. I believe you to be in league with the villain, Todd!

* Alternatively a panel in the wall behind the chair rises and Mark enters from the hidden space.

Tobias No, please, I'm not.

Mark (*still threatening*) What are you doing here, then?

Tobias (*weeping*) I can't get away, he'll kill me if I do!

Mark Why didn't you warn me the other day, eh? You stood watching long enough.

Tobias I did, sir. I did try. But you didn't understand.

Mark Is that what you were up to when you were waving your arms about?

Tobias nods

   (*Less bluntly*) All right, stop crying. No-one's going to hurt you. (*He squats down and hands Tobias a handkerchief*) Here, use this and dry your eyes. (*After a pause*) Where is he now?

Tobias (*pointing*) Seeing Mrs Lovett at the pie-shop.

Mark There? (*He looks*)

Tobias Yes, sir. (*Drying his eyes*) But we must hurry from here, sir, for it's Mr Todd's intention to return with Mrs Lovett.

Mark (*quickly and decisively*) Now listen, Tobias, you'll stay here no longer. Seek out Miss Oakley as quickly as you can. Tell her that I'm still alive, then both of you seek out a magistrate and tell him all that's happened.

Tobias Won't you come with me, sir?

Mark No, the temptation's great, but I must stay here to find out as much as I can about the villain. Now run as if a devil's after you.

Tobias (*running across the shop to the other corridor*) I'll leave this way, sir, as Mr Todd and Mrs Lovett could be coming from her shop at any moment.

Mark Haven't you anything warm to wear?

Tobias No, sir.

Mark (*removing his jacket and buttoning it on Tobias*) Here, wear this. I found it on someone down below, but it won't harm you and it'll keep you warm.

Tobias The Lord protect you, sir.

Tobias exits

Mark (*looking about him*) This man Todd must know of another entrance to the cellar below. I was not alone down there, one or two victims—in the pitch dark it was difficult to know with certainty—already dead, kept me company. Indeed, I fell on a corpse, and that is why I'm not lying there now with a broken neck. But why doesn't he follow his victims to the cellar and make certain of their end? Perhaps he prefers to kill a man who has lain there two days or more rather than go and kill him straight away. Perhaps he feels it's safer lest somebody should still be able to fight him. The rogue—perhaps I should await him there and twist his neck—or should I attempt to discover more about the vaults?

A light appears outside in the street

(*Catching sight of it*) It could be them. I'll return the way I came.

Mark goes to the chair vault and descends. The trap falls into place over him.
A second or so later Sweeney opens the shop door and ushers Mrs Lovett inside. He is holding a lantern

Mrs Lovett I can't see, Todd!

Sweeney It's yer eyes.

Mrs Lovett The way you're holding that lamp, you mean. (*She is miserable and determined not to be good company*)

Sweeney (*putting the lamp on the card table*) Now come along, come along, my lovely, it's Saturday night. Let's have a little game to cheer you up and then an onion sandwich.

Mrs Lovett Oh don't, Todd, don't.

Sweeny Don't you like onion sandwiches? (*He goes to the parlour*)

Mrs Lovett (*sitting at the table and resting her head in her hands*) No, I don't want to play any games.

Sweeney returns with a chair and the game and sits at the table

Not snakes and ladders, anyway. It's a child's game.

Sweeney sets the game out

Nothing can cheer me up. It's the dreams I have. (*Musing*) I want to leave this business and retire. And besides, it ain't a nice business for a lady of my inclinations. I should be living in peace and contentment in a cottage with roses round the door, not slaving away in a dirty cellar making pies! (*Becoming fanciful*) I imagine myself now walking through the fields I knew as a child, in the hay meadows before they were cut, Todd—with the grass as tall as my head, and big moon daisies nodding about me. (*After a pause*) Have you ever seen a moon daisy, Todd? It's petals are lovely and white and it has a nice yellow centre.

Sweeny (*looking at her; sourly*) You been drinking?

Mrs Lovett No, course I ain't. But I could do with a drop!

Sweeney (*rising*) Might cheer you up.

Sweeney goes out to the corridor

Mrs Lovett Been a time since I've had a taste here.

Sweeney returns with a bottle of gin and two glasses

I'm still a country girl at heart, you know, and I can't help being poetical. These city ways are foreign to my nature. Why did I ever come to this sinful city?

Sweeney (*handing her a glass of gin*) Well, you came, didn't you? Don't drink it all at once, big belly!

Mrs Lovett (*putting down the empty glass*) I'll thank you not to call me names.

Sweeney (*handing her the dice shaker*) You can 'ave first shake.

Mrs Lovett (*shaking, then looking miserably at the dice*) Five.

Sweeney Yer can't start.

Mrs Lovett I know!

Sweeney (*shaking*) Six! I'm off! (*Gesticulating*) I'm in me gig—and I'm off!

Mrs Lovett (*muttering*) Wish you were in your coffin. (*She goes to shake*)

Sweeney I've another throw.

Mrs Lovett Go on, then!

Sweeney Six! (*He moves his counter*) Aha! (*Shaking again*) Four! (*Moving the counter*) One, two, three, four—a ladder! A ladder! Up I go! (*He gesticulates excitedly*)

Mrs Lovett (*unhappily*) I haven't started yet. (*She shakes*) Two.

Sweeney You don't shake hard enough. (*He shakes*) Six! (*He shakes again*) Two! (*He moves his counter*) Yah! Yah! (*He sticks out his tongue*) Missed Madam Snake's gaping gob!

Mrs Lovett Don't be nasty, Todd. (*She shakes*) I haven't started yet! One! (*Depressed and angry*) I don't want to play this game. (*She knocks the dice and shaker on the floor*)

Sweeney (*rising and throwing out his arm in anger*) You don't play games with me like this, Lovett!

Mrs Lovett (*rising*) Oh, don't I! (*Savagely*) You always win because you always cheat!

Sweeney (*condescendingly*) I always win because I'm just that bit superior in skill.

Mrs Lovett (*tossing her head and making fun of his sudden "superior" tone*) Oh! I'm mighty superior to this manner of bickering, oh, the Lord love me ribbons I am, Mr Todd. (*In her ordinary voice*) I'm of loftier inclinations than you, in any case, Sweeney Todd. Never have I sunk to your low level of depravity—wearing your victim's clothes!

Sweeney (*snarling*) Only those which wouldn't be recognized, you fool! And you could hardly wear them, could you—all my customers are men.

Mrs Lovett (*stretching out her arms*) Oh, Todd! Todd! We must reform! The wicked manner of our lives darkens every hour and colours all our dreams with blood! (*As if in a trance*) Nothing do we see but piles of corpses and rivers of blood! And above all this filth and dirt a thousand bobby 'owlers fly! And our world's throbbing with poison, Todd. And it's all maggots and nibble and suck.

Sweeney (*regarding her suspiciously*) You haven't been too friendly of late with Lupin, have you?

Mrs Lovett (*confused*) No, of course not.

Sweeney It sounds like his gibberish. You never talked this way before. (*Grasping her wrist*) You haven't, have you? I know how to make you tell the truth.

Mrs Lovett (*defiantly*) No. I told you.

Sweeney (*tightening his grip*) You sure you've not taken a fancy to him and become less fascinated by me? I'm not too ungentlemanly for you, am I?

Mrs Lovett (*whimpering*) Don't, Todd, you're hurting me!

Sweeney Now tell me, my lovely, what's really upset you?

Mrs Lovett William Grant died last night.

Sweeney And who might William Grant be?

Mrs Lovett He was my baker, Mr Todd.

Sweeney But my dear Mrs Lovett, your baker's name was Jones.

Mrs Lovett (*bursting into tears*) He had a nice face, that Jones had, Mr Todd, but he got discontented. Don't you remember?

Sweeney There are so many of them—one gets confused. (*Releasing his grip; kindly*) Dry those tears, cry-baby. (*He puts his arm round her*)

Mrs Lovett (*firmly*) Todd, I tell you now there has to be an end; and I inform you that the pie-shop in Bell Yard is going to be closed. (*She removes his arm and gives him back the handkerchief*) And I tell you, Sweeny Todd, demon in human shape that you are, that you and I shall shortly see the last of each other. (*She moves to go*)

Sweeney (*running between her and the door*) My heart goes out to you in sympathy, Mrs L. (*Menacingly pointing to the barber's chair*) Let me implore you to take a seat.

Mrs Lovett In *that* chair? Do you think I'm such a fool?

Sweeney (*taking her wrists and pulling her towards the chair*) When do you want me to do it? I'll oblige you now! Sit in the chair and I'll slit you from guts to gantry.

Mrs Lovett (*pulling away*) Please, please, Todd, my dear . . .

Sweeney (*pulling her against him and bending one of her arms behind her back*) Believe me, my dear, the management of women is much like the management of horses—force judiciously applied. (*Slowly relaxing his hold and smiling*) But come, let us sit down again and talk like old friends. (*He indicates the chair at the card table*)

Mrs Lovett (*sitting meekly*) Yes, Mr T.

Sweeney (*sitting opposite her*) You know that you do not mean what you just said just now. Come, come, think a little, be reasonable, Mrs T. (*He takes her hand*)

Mrs Lovett Pray leave go my hand. You are crushing it. I can almost hear the bones crackle.

Sweeney (*complacently*) I have always been noted for my strength. (*He releases her hand*)

Mrs Lovett I must go out. I must breathe the clean air.

Sweeney (*rising*) If it's air you want, I'll fan you. (*He fans her vigorously with the Snakes and Ladders board*)

Mrs Lovett (*rising and moving towards the door*) Stop it, sweetheart! I must go outside!

Sweeney (*moving before her, fanning all the time*) I'll fan you! But why this hurry to be out this time of night?

Mrs Lovett Let me by, sweetheart. Let me by, lover. (*She weeps*)

Sweeney Nay, nay, we shall stay here and talk of your troubles. (*After a* *pause*) You were speaking of the unexpected demise of this—let me see, what was his name? Not Jones—what was it now? Ay, cry on, cry on. It'll do you good.

Mrs Lovett (*weeping*) Let me go.

St Dunstan's clock strikes twelve

Sweeney Ah, midnight. Another day's dead and done with. (*Politely curious*) You're not thinking of going now, are you?

Mrs Lovett (*shaking her head*) It's too late now.

She allows Sweeney to lead her back to the card table

It's too late now. (*With another sad shake of her head she sits down*)

Sweeney (*affably*) Yes, I know. You've already said so. (*After a pause*) He'll have gone by now, will he?

Mrs Lovett (*wearily*) What d'you mean, Todd?

Sweeney (*smiling*) Just my little joke. But never mind, let's sit here quietly for a time holding hands——

He places his hands palms upwards on the table, and Mrs Lovett meekly places hers in them

—and then we'll get—amorous. . . .

CURTAIN

SCENE 2

The following afternoon.

Mrs Lovett and Mark Ingestrie enter the bakehouse down the stairs from the pie shop. Mark, unshaven, is obviously pretending to be someone of simpler and cruder nature than himself

Mrs Lovett Since you came here begging for work, and since you're alone in the world and don't look too saucy, I'll give you employment. Your job is the manufacture of pies, the best that can be made, and you'll also be responsible for feeding the fires and making yourself generally useful.

Mark (*finger to brow*) Yes, ma'am.

Mrs Lovett Your garments look as if you were once a naval man, and I warn you that I'm not the sort of woman who extends favours to naval men. Furthermore, I will not tolerate any man taking advantage of the dark corridors and pressing himself against me. The temptation will be great, but you must practice as much control as you can.

Mark (*finger to brow*) Yes, ma'am. (*After a pause*) I suppose I'm to have someone to assist me in this situation. One pair of hands could never do the work in such a place.

Mrs Lovett Are you uncontent already?

Mark No, ma'am. Only you spoke of having a man.

Mrs Lovett Oh, he has gone to his friends and that is how I find myself able to employ you—(*pausing*)—to some of his very oldest friends, who will be glad to see him. Have you any further remarks to make?

Mark Yes, ma'am. I should like to leave when it pleases me.

Mrs Lovett You may make your mind easy on that score. I never keep anybody many hours after they begin to feel they wish to leave. But now I must leave you for a time. As long as you are industrious and capable we will get on well; but as soon as you begin to get idle and neglect my orders you will receive a piece of information that may . . . (*she stops*)

Mark What is it, ma'am? I'm of an enquiring nature, and you might as well tell me now.

Mrs Lovett No. I seldom find there is occasion for it at first; but after a time when you get well fed you are sure to want it. Everybody who relinquishes this situation goes to his old friends—friends that he has not seen for many years! (*She looks at him significantly*) I shall return anon.

Mrs Lovett goes

Mark (*gazing after her*) What a strange manner of talking that middle-aged female has! There seems to be something mysterious in all she utters. I feel sure that she knows what Todd is about, and it is more than sinister that there should be—(*going to the landing and looking down the stairway*)—a secret passage-way between here and Todd's cellar. (*Looking about the bakehouse*) The atmosphere of this place is little better than that cellar, indeed, the smell of the place would be unbearable if it weren't for the delicious odour of the freshly baked pies. (*He goes to the range and picks up a pie*) Delicious! I fancy I could eat one. (*He eats*) Beautiful! Mmm! Lots of gravy and meat. Mmm! (*He suddenly finds a long hair in the pie*) Somebody must have been combing their hair when this was made. What's this? (*He removes a small piece of "something" from his mouth*) A bone? Or is it a finger-nail? Uggh! Uggh! Oh, no! (*He drops the pie and recoils from it*) It can't be—I suddenly feel ill—I want to be . . .

Mark rushes off up the steps to be sick.
A hymn, "Holy, Holy, Holy" is heard being sung off by Sweeney as he climbs the steps from the cellar. When he reaches the landing he stops singing and stares after the direction in which Mark went, wondering who he was. He is wearing a cook's hat and apron and holding to himself a large mixing bowl, which he puts on the table

Sweeney It is a poor man of business who don't know how to make what he sells. (*Starting to put flour and water in the bowl*) And you ain't the only one, lovely Lovett, capable of making a tasty pie. (*He starts to mix and begins to sing "Holy, Holy, Holy" again*) La, la, la, la, lah-la . . . (*He has a good spit into the bowl to aid the mixing*) Holy, Holy, Holy! Oh, oh—oh, oh—ho, ho! (*He stops mixing in order to reflect*) Gathering

C

clouds warn the mountaineer of the approaching storm, let them now warn me to provide against danger. (*He begins to lift the dough out of the bowl and maul it into various shapes. He throws it on the table and begins to roll it, standing back at times to admire his handiwork. He puts a little of the dough in his mouth and chews it*) Most tasty!

Mrs Lovett creeps on to the landing and watches him unobserved

Mmm! Most tasty! (*He swallows the dough and continues to roll it*) Yes, Lovett, your breath smells of pig's chitterlings 'cos you're always eating 'em, and your hair ain't real either. (*After a pause*) Yes, I think the time's come to take control of this side of the business myself.

Mrs Lovett (*drawing a long knife from her dress and muttering to the audience*) You'll feel it where the pain's 'orrible! (*She places the knife in a specially made pocket at the back of her apron, where she can easily reach it, and creeps up behind him*)

Sweeney (*still unaware of her presence*) Yes. I have too many enemies to be safe. I'll dispose of them one by one, until no evidence of my guilt remains. I must find the boy Tobias Ragg and stop his babbling tongue, a close confinement in the asylum of Jonas Fogg will effectually silence him. And with Lovett I'll seize my first opportunity . . .

Mrs Lovett (*suddenly*) Traitor!

Sweeney (*jumping round, startled*) Hum! Ah! Heugh!

Mrs Lovett Since I discover that you intend treachery I shall on the instant demand my share of the booty—aye, an equal share of the fruits of our mutual bloodshed.

Sweeney (*after a pause*) You shall have it.

Mrs Lovett I will have it!

Sweeney (*smirking*) Will?

Mrs Lovett Yes. Every shilling. Every penny!

Sweeney So you shall, if you are only patient. I shall balance accounts with you in a minute. (*He drops the dough back in the bowl, wipes his hands on his apron, and takes an account book from his pocket*)

Mrs Lovett Every shilling!

Sweeney (*after a few moments of reckoning*) Twelve thousand pounds to a fraction.

Mrs Lovett That is just six thousand for each person, there being two of us.

Sweeney Are you sure?

Mrs Lovett That there's two of us?

Sweeney No. Of your arithmetic.

Mrs Lovett (*indignantly*) I can divide by two!

Sweeney But, Mistress Lovett, I must first have you know that before I hand you a coin, you will have to pay me for your support, lodging and clothes.

Mrs Lovett (*astounded*) Clothes?

Sweeney I repeat the word—clothes!

Mrs Lovett Why, I haven't had a new dress this six months!

Sweeney Besides, am I to have nothing for your education? Who taught you how to use a knife on an over-curious assistant? And who offered to give you total protection and provision for all these years? And after deducting that and the expense of erecting furnaces, purchasing flour for your delicious pies, etc., I find it leaves a balance of sixteen shillings fourpence and three-farthings in my favour—(*wagging the account book in front of her nose*)—and I don't intend to budge an inch until it is paid.

Mrs Lovett (*coldly at first, but becoming more enraged as she continues*) You want to rob me; but you shall find to your sorrow that I will have my due! (*She draws out her knife*)

Sweeney steps back in alarm

Now, villain, who triumphs? Put your name to a deed consigning the whole of the wealth blood has purchased or you perish where you stand! Hurry. (*She brandishes the knife*)

Sweeney starts backing round the table

For I'd dearly like to draw your blood to cleanse my memory of the foul lechery you've forced on me in Buttercup Yard!

Sweeney backs away, Mrs Lovett pursuing stealthily

Yes, Todd, your usage of my gorgeous body has come to an end. Your leasehold has ended for I seek better occupants—sweet-smelling as new-mown hay, lively as crickets. (*Waving the knife and yelling*) I'll carve you to tatters, you unkempt midden! Smell of chitterlings, do I? What will you smell of—your blood and tripes squelching under my feet?

She rushes at him, but he dodges her

My limbs are lovely, my legs are lovely—not begrimed with the filth of years, misbegotten sinner of evil and inquity. Let the old serpent of Hell crawl over my guts, but I'll have my revenge on you! I'll cut your fixtures and fittings to tatters, and finish you off once and for all, here and now. (*She rushes at him*)

Sweeney (*hurling a large roll of dough at her*) Will you, my dear? Take that!

He rushes and struggles with her for the knife. Grasping and squeezing her wrist, he forces her to drop it. She dashes for the entrance. He has placed his foot on the knife, but now leaves it and dashes after her, grabbing her from behind. Lifting her bodily, he throws her back into the room. She lands near the knife, but before she can grab hold of it he places his foot on it again. As he bends to pick it up she scrambles on all fours away from him, her eyes wide with fear

(*Brandishing the knife*) I'll tickle your kidneys! (*Standing over her*) Your last hour has come—now say your prayers!

Mrs Lovett (*seizing hold of his legs and hauling herself into a kneeling position*) Spare my life for the love of Heaven, as I spared yours. You cannot have the heart to kill me. (*Holding his knife away from her with her arms*) I will not loose my hold.

He tries to push her off

You cannot throw me off.

Squeezing her neck with his free hand he manages to hurl her back from him

Oh stop, stop before you spill my blood. I have been true to you, upon my guilty soul! (*She throws herself about his legs again*)

Sweeney (*trying to step back*) Off! Off!

Mrs Lovett (*clinging to him on her knees*) Oh, Todd, Todd, I won't be a miserable cry-baby any more. I'll be content and play games with you, and cook your pies and be a comfort to you.

Sweeney stabs her in the back and she drops at his feet

Sweeney Perdition, if I let you keep on someone will be coming in! (*He removes the knife, places it on the table, and stares at his hands*) There is blood upon my hands. (*He looks at her*) And she is dead. (*He removes the tray of pies from the top of the oven and places it against the oven door*)

Smoke and flame arise from the top of the oven. Sweeney drags Mrs Lovett's body to it and begins to slide and lower her into the smoke and flames head first. Her legs are left sticking out from the top while he finds a poker to poke her down

(*Standing back from his poking*) Now let the furnace consume the body as it would wheaten straw, and destroy all evidence of my guilt in this as it has in my manifold deeds of blood. (*As he finishes poking her down he begins to hum and sing "Abide with me, fast falls the eventide". He replaces the poker, warms his hands, then removes his apron, puts it on a chair, wipes the knife and places it on the range. He continues to hum and sing as he gazes down at the fire*)

Curtain

Scene 3

The same. Several hours later
Sweeney is seated at the table with his head and arms lying across it. He is asleep, a half-empty whisky bottle by his hand. There is silence for several moments, then out of this silence an eerie voice is heard calling from above the stage

Voice (*eerily*) Sweeney Todd! (*After a pause*) Sweeney Todd! (*After a pause*) Sweeney Todd!

Sweeney moves restlessly

Sweeney Todd!

Sweeney (*awakening slowly, and yawning*) I must have fallen asleep after poppin' 'er in. (*Looking about*) It's gone cold in 'ere. (*He rises*) Funny, strange place, this. I hope Lovett don't come back and 'aunt me! (*He laughs*) I remember now, I've been dreaming. (*He drinks from the whisky bottle*) Dreaming of my youth and my first murder. I was eighteen, and on my way walking to London I was thirsty. And I asked for a drink of water at a cottage door from an old lady and gentleman who lived there. They gave me the water and then I cut their throats and buried them in the wallflower bed. The smell of those flowers is with me still. (*He delicately sniffs the air about him*)

Voice (*calling*) Sweeney Todd!

Sweeney (*looking up*) Eh, what's that?

Voice Sweeney Todd!

Sweeney (*eagerly*) Eh! Eh! Are you the voices from above?

Voice No, we are the ones from below!

Sweeney (*smirking*) Oh, you've got little 'orns, have you? And little curly tails? Well, I don't want to talk to you. (*He pauses*) Is it warm where you are?

Voice Yes.

Sweeney Are you with anybody I know?

Voice No.

Sweeney (*irritably*) What you want of me, then?

Voice We have come for you.

Sweeney Oh, 'ave you! Well, you don't scare me! No, you can keep on blabbin' all night, but you don't scare me! (*He pauses*) There's only one thing which does.

Voice What is it?

Sweeney Ah! Haha! Interested, aren't you?

Voice Yes. (*After a pause*) What is it?

Sweeney Shan't tell you.

Voice What is it?

Sweeney Footsteps! Like this! (*He walks about, making exaggerated steps*) Boom! Tread! Tread! (*He stops and looks towards the entrance, pretending he sees someone there. Pulling back*) And slowly he walks towards you . . .

Voice Like this?

There is the sound of hollow ghostly steps from above

Sweeney (*frightened*) No! No! (*Peering at the entrance across the room*) Oh, I can see you. I've seen you before on rainy days in old grey streets, and I've seen you coming out of cemetery gates wearing a cloak and a big top hat, all bent up 'cos you're a withered old devil and your tongue sticks out of your mouth like a bit of grey bacon—come on, let's be seeing you!

Creaking steps are heard coming down the stairs

(*His head thrust forward, listening*) I can 'ear you—creak—creak . . . (*He breaks off*)

A figure appears in the gloom on the landing

(*His hands held out in terror*) Keep away! Keep away! You dead, 'orrible, dirty, stinkin' 'orror!

The figure enters the room with a dark sheet wrapped around it. Sweeney cringes in terror. Slowly the figure removes the sheet and Sweeney sees Mark Ingestrie standing before him

(*Howling with rage and relief*) Yah! (*After a long pause*) So it's you, is it? I should have polished you off with the knife, except I thought you'd still be lying moaning and groaning, that's if you weren't already "dyead"—and I'd come along and tell you how I was going to slice your nose off your pretty countenance, and cut your strong young throat before carting you off to Lovett's to be made into nourishment for the local populace. You must have fallen well, you nimble son of fast and furious fornication! Ha! Ha! I'm crude, ain't I? Depraved, eh? I've left some of 'em lying in my vault for a week, and when I've gone to finish 'em off all I've 'ad to do is 'it them on the 'ead with a 'ammer. (*Shaking his head*) Some of the poor souls die of heart attack. But don't it smell, eh, don't it smell down there? Haha!

Mark You're to be brought to justice, Todd.

Sweeney (*mockingly*) Oh, surely not! Me? What have I done wrong? I'm innocent, my lud! (*Becoming enraged*) Not by you, I won't! I'm strong. Strong, me lad. I'll break you in half first.

Mark That boy Tobias will have seen Joanna Oakley and they'll have seen a magistrate by now.

Sweeney Thank you. When I've finished with you, I've every intention of having him snuffed. I'll have him confined up in the asylum. Jonas Fogg is always willing to oblige. (*To the audience*) I've never been able to kill children myself. Funny, isn't it? I'm too romantic. (*To Mark*) I get 'em put in the asylum and Fogg lets 'em live for a few months and then they die mysteriously, and he buries them privately himself. I wouldn't be a bit surprised if he didn't poison 'em, he's that sort of villain, you know.

Mark (*with cold hatred*) Todd!

Sweeney (*mockingly*) What is it, my dear? Your Miss Oakley and her magistrate will never come searching for us here, you know.

Mark I'm glad of that, Todd, 'cos I want to kill you—kill you with my bare hands. (*He crouches ready to attack Sweeney*)

Sweeney (*spitting on the palms of his hands*) That's the talk, me lad. Come on then, my hearty. A real hero, ain't you? (*He circles about the room*) Fortune's darling, I'll enjoy kicking you into pig's dripping!

Sweeney dashes at Mark, who turns aside, and backs toward the ovens. Sweeney strikes with his fist but Mark dodges it. Sweeney strikes again and Mark avoids it once more, but this time he hits Sweeney in the stomach and then, as Sweeney crumples, shoots his right fist under his jaw. Sweeney hurtles back and falls full length on the floor. He lies there groaning

Oh, oh—my—my—oh, oh . . .

Mark (*moving close to him and eyeing him suspiciously*) You're not finished yet?

Sweeney Oooh, I am. (*He twists about the floor in spasms of agony*) I am —for ever—I can't move . . .

Mark You're lying!

Sweeney (*wailing*) I'm an old man—oooh, aagh—the pain . . .

Mark (*bending down*) What is it . . .

Sweeney punches Mark with great force in the face and stomach. Mark is hurled back, and Sweeney with great speed rushes him against the wall by the ovens and bangs his head against the wall until he is senseless. Sweeney lets go of him, and Mark drops to the floor. Sweeney drags him to the centre of the floor and goes to stamp on his face, but stays himself

Sweeney No. I won't finish you off. Not yet. Not until I've brought Miss Oakley here to see you. Let's have that belt. (*He removes Mark's trousers belt and binds his ankles together with it*) Then you can both watch Sweeney have a bit of fun. You're a handsome pair of turtle-doves, well-grouped, but Sweeney will show you that it ain't only a clear eye and a goodly build which is of account in this world, my lad. There's such a thing as power, my hearty, crude, cunning, wicked power —and I've got the better of you there. Eh? Eh? Now this. (*He takes Mark's kerchief and binds his hands behind his back*) I'll execute your wildest juicy sailor dreams with our virgin, Miss Oakley, right in this bakehouse, right in front of your eyes. Yes, I'll go out and find Miss Oakley, but I don't know which of you I'll polish off first—you or her? (*He scratches his head, then tests the knots*) There, that's satisfactory. Yes, I'd like to kill you, then her. (*He drags Mark to the ovens so that his head and shoulders are resting in the angle formed by the ovens and the wall*) Then you again. Then her again. Then you, and so on. (*He takes another swig of whisky*) Him, her, him, her, him, her, him, her. (*Becoming agitated, and drumming his fingers on the table*) Yes, I'll go out in the streets now—(*to the audience, a fanatical look in his eyes*)—and all you lusty young loving couples, watch out! Sweeney is on the prowl! And I hate yer. It'll be you, then her. Eh? Eh? Haha! All you young fellows with fancy notions in your heads, wenching in shop doorways, in narrow alleyways, yearning for it under the arch of a bridge—watch out tonight, 'cos old Sweeney is on the loose and he'll uncouple you. (*He moves towards the exit*) I'll put an end to all this recreation and fun and games. (*He turns back in the exit*) I'll finish the lot of you and pack you off to Paradise. (*He looks steadily at the audience then rushes up the steps with his razor in his hand*) I'm after you!

The LIGHTS *change. Street noises and a newspaper boy's voice can be heard. There is the sound of a barrel-organ playing, people passing by, horse-drawn cabs, drays, gay and screeching laughter, then the scene settles down to the mood and atmosphere of a quiet, narrow alley at night. Lights focus on the alley and steps, and the newsboy calls out clearly from the quiet*

Newspaper Boy (*off*) Murder! Murder! Ha'penny a sheet! All details! Maniac at large!

Voices are heard passing by

> *A young couple enter. They are both simply dressed in working-class clothes of the period. Flo wears a long dress with underskirts and a shawl around her shoulders. Henry is dressed in plain-coloured trousers, a woollen jersey, kerchief and cap. He carries a short jacket over his arm. He stops to look in the pie-shop window*

Flo (*tugging him*) Come on, Henry, don't stay about 'ere—we'll be murdered.
Henry (*cuddling her*) You ain't scared with me, are you, Flo? (*He laughs*) Eh?
Flo This is the street Ma was telling us about.
Henry (*cheerfully*) No, it ain't.
Flo Yes, it is.
Henry Just another kiss.
Flo No.

He kisses her

(*Protesting mildly*) Oh, Henry!
Henry There. No-one will attack you with me around. Come on, give us another.
Flo (*looking across at Sweeney's door*) Over there—in the shadows—what is it?
Henry Where?
Flo There!
Henry Some bloke! Eh! You! (*He goes to Sweeney's shop door*)

The shape of a man, Sweeney, is seen through the shop window
There is hardly any struggle. Sweeney makes a sharp movement towards Henry's neck. Henry grunts and staggers, collapsing slowly out of sight in front of the shop door

Flo (*petrified*) Henry! (*She pauses*) Henry! Is it you?

Sweeney looms over her and brings her body against his for a moment, then releases her. She staggers against the wall and slowly collapses

> *Sweeney opens his shop door, walks down through the dark of the shop and exits through the parlour*
> *Joanna enters the alleyway*

Joanna (*weeping*) Mark! Mark! (*She stumbles over Flo's body and saves herself from falling down the steps by holding on to the side of the pie-shop window*) Oh, my ankle! Oh, I've—my ankle . . . (*She carefully tries to place her foot to the ground*)

Flo, as she lies dying, coughs

Flo (*pulling herself up against the wall*) Help me! Help me!
Joanna (*trying to bend down to comfort Flo*) What is it?
Flo Tell my ma . . . (*Her voice breaks off*)
Joanna (*feeling blood on her hand*) Blood! (*Replacing her hand comfortingly on Flo's shoulder*) You'll be all right. Never mind. (*After a pause*) She's dead.

The pie-shop door opens and a man appears

Oh, sir, please help!

The man is seen to be Sweeney

Sweeney What is it, my dear?
Joanna (*screaming as she hears his voice*) No! (*She struggles down the alley steps but collapses at the bottom in great pain*)
Sweeney My turtle-dove—caught! (*He laughs as he bends to pick her up, but is stopped by voices*)
Voices (*off*) Good night, Mr Fogg. Good night, Mr Fogg.
Fogg (*off*) Sssh! Sssh!
Voice (*off*) Good night, Mr Fogg.

Fogg appears at the far end of the alley

Fogg (*nervously, with his finger to his lips*) Sssh! (*He picks his way carefully down the alley, stepping round Flo's body and on down the steps. He is a fastidious man in his late fifties or early sixties. He wears a top hat, frock coat and pantaloons, or trousers fitted under the shoe, and carries gloves and a stick*)
Sweeney (*looking out of the dark*) Ah, Jonas Fogg.
Fogg (*with a gasp of fear and surprise*) Aaah!
Sweeney My superior friend, you've bungled everything!
Fogg (*trying to be casual*) Is that you, Mr Todd? (*Laughing*) You are, if my memory does not deceive me. Haha!
Sweeney (*unpleasantly*) Haha! I believe I'm not easily forgotten by those who have once seen me, Fogg.
Fogg Yes, you have a memorable face.
Sweeney The face of a man with a tile loose, perhaps?
Fogg Oh no, no, no, no. Of course not. Tch, tch, tch. Really, Todd, what a strange idea.
Sweeney You've bungled everything, you blown-up ferret!
Fogg (*protesting with raised hand*) No, Todd, I haven't. Believe me, my good fellow, I haven't. It's none of my fault at all. (*Touching Sweeney with his stick*) And remember, Todd, you've had a—a strenuous day, and your judgement is, perhaps, falling short of its usual infallibility. But, Todd, are you aware that the constabulary are out looking for you? Truly, you'd best go and hide.
Sweeney (*grabbing hold of Fogg's lapels*) Why, you rat, you'd set 'em on me the first chance you get! Why ain't you been to see me earlier? That Tobias should have been seen to by you as soon as he left my place!

D

Fogg He was with Joanna Oakley. She would not hand him over to me.

Sweeney Don't you believe in forceful persuasion?

Fogg It was out of the question, Todd. She's seen too many people.

Sweeney Well, she's let go of him now, anyway, she's there on the ground. (*Tightening his grip*) You couldn't bother to help truly, could you, Fogg? You'd like to see me swing 'cos I know far more about your way of business than is 'ealthy for you, don't I? How many children you spiflicated in that "insteetootshun" of yours?

Fogg (*with a stamp and a rap of his stick on the ground*) That's a serious accusation, Todd!

Sweeney (*drily*) Oh, is it? I am sorry. I withdraw it completely. (*He takes Fogg's stick*) What a splendid stick. Mmm. Very fine. As a matter of speculation, do you think you could break a stick like this, Fogg?

Fogg (*humouring him*) Oh, haha, I shouldn't think so. Physical exertion's not a strong point.

Sweeney (*handing him the stick*) Go on. Try. (*Menacingly*) If you don't break it, I'll break you.

Fogg (*laughing desperately as he tries to break the stick*) Oh, haha now, Todd, do be serious, haha.

Sweeney I am. Try harder.

Fogg (*trying*) I—I can't. I knew I couldn't.

Sweeney (*taking the stick*) What a shame. What a pity. Never mind. I was only joking.

Fogg (*retreating*) You must excuse me now, Todd. I'm so glad I've found you and told you what I could. I must be retracing my steps, however.

Sweeney Going to find a constable, are you?

Fogg No, of course not!

Sweeney In that case I'll stroll along with you a bit of the way. Up 'ere then, you say?

Fogg nods, and he and Sweeney stroll off

(*As they go*) Streets are quiet tonight. (*He pauses*) Why, why don't you say something? (*Another pause*) Few people about . . .

Fogg and Sweeney go off. There is a pause, then the noise of three or four blows of the stick as Sweeney attacks Fogg. Fogg's screams are heard. Then Sweeney walks back on again, alone, carrying a broken stick which he drops at the top of the steps

(*Picking up Joanna*) You'll soon see someone who's been longing to see you. (*He carries Joanna through his shop door*)

Joanna (*murmuring*) Where are we? (*She suddenly begins to struggle wildly, but after a few moments sinks down into his arms again, exhausted*) Where are we?

Sweeney (*as he carries her down into the darkness of his shop*) You'll soon find out. (*He laughs*)

Sweeney sings "Sweet Lass of Richmond Hill", "Drink to me only with

*thine eyes" or some similar traditional air as he carries Joanna off
through the parlour*

The LIGHTS *fade on the alley and go up on the bakehouse, where Mark is
lying bound as before*

*Sweeney is heard singing and humming as he carries Joanna on to the
landing, as if he had brought her up from the cellar below the bakehouse.
He places her down so that she is lying against Mark*

Sweeney There! (*He stands upright*) Forgive the bareness of the bridal
chamber.

Sweeney goes off as if down to the cellars and returns with a thin mattress

Joanna (*slowly recognizing Mark*) Mark! Mark!

Mark (*very weak, with a trickle of dried blood on his face; barely audibly*)
Joanna . . .

Sweeney Is that all you can say to one another? Tch! Tch! I'll bind your
ankle before polishing you off. (*He puts the mattress on the floor, then
goes to the table and pours some whisky on a rag he takes from his pocket.
He binds Joanna's ankle*) What interests me, my dear, is why you aren't
sweet to me and beg me not to operate on you. I'd do anything for you,
my dear. (*Indicating Mark*) You see, I've kept him alive, I ain't even cut
out his tongue. (*He carries Joanna to the mattress*) Now this is where I'll
finish you off nice and gentle when I've had my will of you——

Mark (*barely audible*) Todd . . .

Sweeney —in the middle of my transports of passion I'll stifle you and
stick a knife in your guts, you won't know you've had it, so much will
be happening to you. (*He places her carefully on the mattress*) Then I'll
carry your lover across and sprinkle his blood over you. Why don't you
uncover your beauty for me, my Venus? You must often have thought
of uncovering yourself—that first night after holy wedlock when it's
decreed that pale flesh shall cleave—and sport is naked and unashamed.
(*He removes his waistcoat and drops it to the ground as he kneels beside
her*) Why is it, my dear, that a young buck like that—(*indicating Mark*)
—can play the Adam and I can only play—the fool? (*Half lifting her in
his arms*) I ain't ever held a beauty like you in my arms before, Joanna
Oakley. (*He pauses*) Say you love me, Joanna Oakley.

Joanna turns her head from him

Say you love me!

*She keeps her head averted. In the distance can be heard the baying of hounds
and the blowing of a police whistle*

They're howling for my blood—but they won't be in time to save you—
no, Sweeney will see to that! (*He lowers Joanna on to the mattress then
moves to Mark, picking up Mrs Lovett's knife from the range on his way*)
You love this fellow, don't you?

Joanna (*half crawling to the table to support her as she tries to stand*)
Please, please, Mr Todd, kill me if you must, but stop torturing me!
Sweeney You love this fellow, don't you?
Joanna (*weeping and in despair*) Yes, yes, yes!
Sweeney Now say you love me! Say it!
Joanna I can't!
Sweeney (*threatening her with the knife*) Say you love me though I'm
vicious, depraved and ugly!
Joanna (*wildly*) I can't! I can't! Kill me! Kill me!
Sweeney No, damn you! Damn you! But I'll do for him! (*To Mark*) Your
whore can watch the blade go in and your blood fly! Now! Now! (*In a
paroxysm of rage and self-pity he cuts through the air with the knife as
if killing Mark*)

Joanna moves wildly and imploringly to Sweeney

Now! Now! Now! Now!   ⎫ *speaking*
Joanna No! No! Please, please don't kill him! *Don't!* ⎰ *together*

Joanna screams. There is silence for a moment

(*Weeping*) I'm so afraid of you. (*Distraught*) Afraid! And I love Mark
and I don't know what can be done—because I don't love you—I don't
—I don't—I feel sorrow for you—a terrible sorrow—I . . .

*Joanna breaks off as she realizes that her arms are thrown out impulsively
towards Sweeney and that there are tears on Sweeney's face*

(*Gently*) What is it?

Sweeney (*moving to her*) Just one kiss. (*He pauses*) Just the one kiss which
has been denied me all my life—(*hesitantly*)—that pure kiss which pene-
trates the soul!
Mark (*murmuring*) Joanna!

*Joanna kisses Sweeney. He goes on his knees and presses his face against
her waist. There is a sound of a window being smashed, and lights appear in
the parlour corridor of Sweeney's shop: then the sound of heavy footsteps,
as if rapid searching is going on. Sweeney rises and, after gazing at Joanna,
goes and slashes through Mark's bonds.*

Two men make their way down the alley and rap on the pie-shop door

*Sweeney moves down stage. Mark holds Joanna, restraining her from going
to Sweeney*

Joanna (*realizing what Sweeney is about to do*) No . . .
Sweeney How cruel and beautiful is life! (*He plunges the dagger into his
stomach and drops to his knees, his body folding up*)

*The men burst through the pie-shop door and race down the stairs into
the bakehouse. They wear capes and top hats. One carries a pistol*

A Man Where is he?

Mark and Joanna make no reply, but gaze helplessly at Sweeney crumpled on his knees, dying

(*Following their gaze*) Sweeney Todd, villain, I have a warrant for your arrest!

Sweeney (*lifting himself up, pulling the knife from his wound, and staggering towards the Man with the blade upraised*) Damn yer eyes!

The Man fires the pistol, and Sweeney, throwing his arms in the air, crumples to his knees. After a moment the knife falls from his fingers. Joanna rushes forward weeping, and manages to arrest part of his fall. Sweeney's fingers cling to her skirt, but first the one hand and then the other slither down. Just before this happens, however, he manages to speak

How cruel and beautiful is life! (*His head drops to his arm and he lies face downwards, stretched out at full length, dead*)

Joanna kneels and, lifting his right hand, holds it to her tear-stained cheek. The LIGHTS *dim except for one spot shining on Joanna. This slowly fades, as—*

the CURTAIN *falls*

THE TRAPDOOR CHAIR

The chair should of course tip the victim downwards through a trap in the stage to a well-padded undercroft. If for any reason this is not possible the following methods could be used.

1. *If there is no undercroft the chair and the immediate area about it could be raised on rostra; the chair placed sideways to audience* (See diagram 1).

A section of the platform top could be hinged to as to form a lid which can be raised and lowered. A metal eye is then screwed into the upstage end of this lid, and a strong thin length of wire passing over a single series of pulleys hooked to it. The other end of the wire is fastened to a cleat hook or winch in the wings. In this way the wooden lid can be raised and lowered at the appropriate time.

Note, however, that the lid is raised towards the audience thus hiding the shallowness of the fall, and that as the lid is rising Sweeney tips the chair (also hinged: see diagram 2) towards the gap and the victim is "hurtled" into the space below. Here he can lie concealed until the end of the scene.

When the victim has been tumbled into the trap the lid is lowered. Sweeney then unhooks the wire and winds it about a cleat hook on the shop wall. There it will appear as a blind-pull for a ceiling window.

Note also that a useful time for the whole procedure to start is when Mark is lying back in the chair with his face lathered and, perhaps, lost in thought. At such a moment Sweeney whilst walking around Mark unwinds the wire from the cleat hook and joins it to the metal eye in the platform. Sound effects should begin a moment or so afterwards. Of course, this means that Sweeney does not leave the stage.

2. *Where there is no undercroft and the rostra system is unsuitable.*

The chair is firmly screwed to a $\frac{3}{4}$-in. plywood base which in turn is screwed to a platform extending 6 in. or so beyond scenery line. The platform needs to measure approximately 4 in. deep, 4 ft. long and $2\frac{1}{2}$ ft. wide (see diagram 3)

Stage rollers or castors are fixed under the platform and the whole can be drawn along specially made wooden tracks through a sliding wall-trap.

This sliding trap consists of a section of a flat which can be raised either simply by hand or by a rope and pulley method. The hand method requires two stage crew, one either side of the section, to push it upwards, sliding it along two runners. The rope and pulley method needs two single pulleys fixed into beams above the stage area and two ropes fixed to the top of the section, one either side, passing over the pulleys and tied to cleat hooks.

It is important for the trap to be lowered once the chair and victim have passed through so that the yells, etc., of the victim falling into a cellar can be performed unseen. This having finished, the platform can move back on to stage; the trap rising to allow the empty chair through and dropping again immediately afterwards. Obviously, all pushing and pulling of the platform can be carried out "invisibly" by stage crew.

3. *Where systems 1 and 2 above cannot be used.*

(*a*) Sweeney either knocks out victim with a blow on the head or strangles him into a state of unconsciousness with a towel. He then lifts a trapdoor by hand and drops the victim into a vault. Having lowered trapdoor he stands on stage chuckling and rubbing his hands together.

(*b*) Sweeney either knocks out victim with a blow on the head or strangles him into a state of unconsciousness with a towel. He then drags him to a wall, pulls a strange lever or presses part of a panel and a trapdoor opens. After the victim has been hurled into a bloodstained vault and the trapdoor has returned to position, Sweeney stands on stage chuckling and rubbing his hands together.

Ian Glenn, Austin Rosser

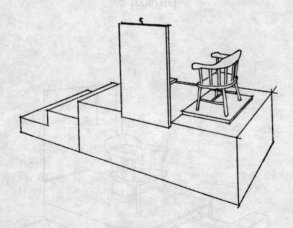

DIAGRAM 1

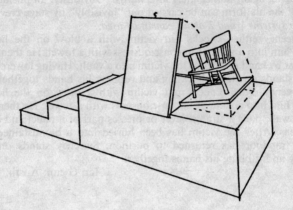

DIAGRAM 2

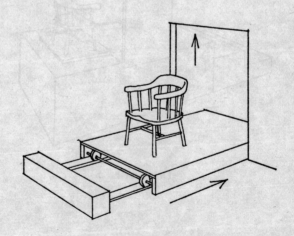

DIAGRAM 3

FURNITURE AND PROPERTY LIST

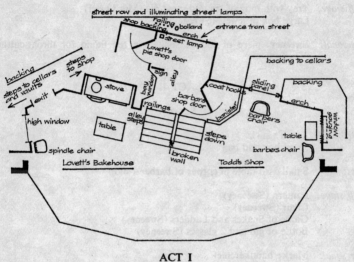

ACT I

SCENE 1

On stage: BARBER SHOP:
Wash-stand. *On it:* water jug, bowl, shaving mug and brush, soap
dish, razor, strop, hairbrush, hand glass. *In drawer:* black velvet or
leather bag of jewels
Barber's chair on trapdoor. *Over arm:* barber's sheet
Wooden chair
Container for walking-sticks
On wall: coat hooks, news sheet
Window curtains
Curtain over parlour opening

BAKEHOUSE:
Kitchen table
Kitchen range. *Beside it:* poker
Wooden chair

Off stage: Bundle of clothes (**Tobias**)
Small kit-bag (**Mark**)

Personal: **Mark:** coin, jewel casket with pearls
Sweeney: coins

SCENE 2

Personal: **Lupin:** brandy flask
           Sweeney: razor

SCENE 3

Off stage: Tray with mug of tea and meat pie **(Mrs Lovett)**
           Large box of jewels **(Sweeney)**

Personal: **Sweeney:** piece of sponge soaked in red liquid for throat-cutting
           effect

ACT II

SCENE 1

Strike: Lupin's stick
           Jewel box and bag

Set: Small card table in corner of barber's shop

Off stage: Lantern **(Sweeney)**
           Chair **(Sweeney)**
           Game of Snakes and Ladders **(Sweeney)**
           Bottle of gin and 2 glasses **(Sweeney)**

Personal: **Mark:** handkerchief
           Sweeney: handkerchief

SCENE 2

Set: Rolling-pin and water jug on bakehouse table
           Small jug of flour under table
           Tray of pies on bakehouse range

Off stage: Mixing bowl and spoon **(Sweeney)**

Personal: **Sweeney:** cook's hat and apron, pocket book
           Mrs Lovett: large knife with retractable blade and blood effect, apron
           with special knife pocket

SCENE 3

Set: Whisky bottle on bakehouse table
           Chair above bakehouse table

Off stage: Thin mattress **(Sweeney)**
           Pistol **(Man)**

Personal: **Sweeney:** razor, rag

LIGHTING PLOT

Property fittings required: gas bracket in barber's shop (optional); hanging
lantern in bakehouse
Interior. A composite set, also showing alleyway.

ACT I, SCENE 1. Morning

To open: Effect of sun spots in barber's shop. Misty on street

Cue 1	**Tobias** enters *Bring up slowly to full morning light*	(Page 1)
Cue 2	**Sweeney:** "No, I'm closed" *Black-Out*	(Page 9)

ACT I, SCENE 2. Night

To open: Effect of fog, dim street lamps and patchy pools on alley

Cue 3	**Sweeney:** "At your service, sir" *Fade to Black-Out*	(Page 13)

ACT I, SCENE 3. Afternoon

To open: General daylight effect, concentrated mainly on barber shop

Cue 4	**Lupin:** "No, no, Todd, please" *Dim lighting until figures appear only in outline*	(Page 22)
Cue 5	After the murder *Bring up lighting to about ½ previous*	(Page 22)
Cue 6	**Sweeney:** ". . . so that I could cut it" *Fade to Black-Out*	(Page 22)

ACT II, SCENE 1. Night

To open: Gas bracket lit in barber shop. Moonlight in alley and through
windows

Cue 7	**Sweeney:** ". . . we'll get—amorous . . ." *Fade to Black-Out*	(Page 28)

ACT II, SCENE 2. Late afternoon

To open: Lantern and stove lit in bakehouse. Cold grey afternoon light
elsewhere

Cue 8	**Mrs Lovett** is pushed into oven *Red glow from oven*	(Page 32)
Cue 9	At end of scene *Fade to glow on Sweeney, then Black-Out*	(Page 32)

ACT II, SCENE 3. Night

To open: Very dim, eerie light in bakehouse. Spot on Sweeney

Cue 10	**When Voices start**	(Page 32)
	Slow build up to previous scene, but without stove or daylight outside	
Cue 11	**Sweeney: "I'm after you!"**	(Page 35)
	Fade to Black-Out	
Cue 12	**As street effects die away**	(Page 35)
	Slow build to dim, shadowy night lighting in alley and street, without street lamp	
Cue 13	**Sweeney carries Joanna off**	(Page 38)
	Fade to Black-Out, then to Cue 10 lighting	
Cue 14	**At end of scene**	(Page 41)
	Fade to spot on Joanna, then to Black-Out	

EFFECTS PLOT

ACT I

Scene 1

Cue 1   After Sweeney exits   (Page 6)
Whirring of cog-wheels and grating of gears for chair effect

Scene 2

Cue 2   At start of scene   (Page 9)
Ship's hooter moans

Scene 3

No cues

ACT II

Scene 1

Cue 3   **Tobias:** ". . . bring me some clothes"   (Page 23)
Chair effect as Cue 1

Cue 4   **Mrs Lovett:** "Let me go"   (Page 28)
St Dunstan's Clock strikes twelve

Scene 2

No cues

Scene 3

Cue 5   **Sweeney:** "I'm after you"   (Page 35)
Various street sounds, passers-by, horses, cabs, drays, barrel-organ, laughter. Continue until transformation completed

Cue 6   **Sweeney:** "Say you love me"   (Page 37)
Baying hounds and police whistle

Cue 7   **Joanna** kisses Sweeney   (Page 40)
Glass crash and sound of heavy footsteps